CALLING ALL ARTISTS

WHY THERE'S NEVER BEEN A BETTER TIME TO BE A CREATIVE

TODD HAMPSON

TIMBUKTOONS PRESS

CALLING ALL ARTISTS:

Why There's Never Been A Better Time To Be A Creative

Todd Hampson

Copyright © 2014 by Todd Hampson

All Rights Reserved

ISBN: 978-1505678765

Version 1.1

Copyeditor: Tracey Hampson

Cover Design/Interior Design: Todd Hampson

Final Layout: Sel P

Published in the United States by Timbuktoons Press

BLURBS

An immensely practical guide for the creative in all of us. Todd Hampson's work has blessed me and thousands of others - his writing about the nuts and bolts of being a working creative will bless many more. Highly recommended!

— **Phil Vischer**, Creator of *VeggieTales* and *What's in the Bible?*

When someone with Todd Hampson's credentials and experience talks about creativity, I listen. In fact, his new book, "Calling All Artists" was the kick in the pants I needed to move forward on my next project. If you live a creative life (and all of us should), then I recommend the book. You won't regret it.

— **Phil Cooke**, filmmaker, media consultant, and author of
One Big Thing: Discovering What You Were Born to Do

Having been an adjunct professor in the cinema and media departments of two major universities, I know firsthand the positive impact this book will have on students. Whether graduating from college or deciding what to do with your life, this book answers hard questions, provides insightful information, and gives you life changing tips on how to make better choices and start a creative career in the 21st century.

— *Kathleen Cooke*, *kathleencooke.com*,
Co-Founder Cooke Pictures, *cookepictures.com*

Todd Hampson's "Calling All Artists" e-book is a GREAT tool for anyone just getting into animation or even those that have been in it awhile and want to reinvent themselves and/or reignite their passions. As artists, we are not very good at looking internally or into the future, so planning our careers is a mysterious journey. Todd really gets you to organize your thoughts and aline them with your talents! That is THE path to success for any artist! Additionally, his optimistic viewpoint toward the industry, and his excitement about it, is a breath of fresh air we all need to hear!

– **Tom Bancroft,** former *Disney* Supervising Animator, director, studio owner, character designer, author

Todd Hampson listens and delivers! I have personally had the privilege of working with Todd and his company Timbuktoons developing an animated series for kids. He and his wonderful team were able to grant my every wish, and then some. The information he shares in this book will absolutely help artists on their creative journey.

– **Cassie Byram,** actress, singer, song-writer, and Executive Creative Producer, *Oodles World Inc.*

ABOUT THE AUTHOR

*You are never too old to set another goal or
to dream a new dream.*

C.S. Lewis

Todd Hampson is a husband, father, and the founder of Timbuktoons, LLC. He has worked for clients such as Phil Vischer (Creator of *Veggie Tales* and *What's In The Bible?*), Saddleback Church, Willow Creek Association, LifeChurch.tv, Orange, BigStuf Camps, ABC's *Extreme Makeover: Home Edition* and has pitched shows to Cartoon Network, Disney Television Animation, Nickelodeon, The Hub, BBC/CBBC/ CBeebies, and PBS Kids. He is a member of the Creative Talent Network and the Illustrator's Club of MD/DC/VA. Todd attended the Corcoran College of Art and Design in Washington, DC. and completed his Bachelor's Degree in Art (with an Art History minor) at the University of Maryland. He is a Metro DC transplant living in Augusta, GA and is involved in his community by serving on a local school council, and has served on creative, KidMin, missions, and leadership teams in churches for over 15 years.

Table of Contents

Who's This Book For and What's It About?

Tell me and I forget, teach me and I may remember,
involve me and I learn.

Benjamin Franklin

I am not a teacher, but an awakener.

Robert Frost

Who Is This Book For?

I am a husband, father, and the founder of Timbuktoons, LLC., an animation and creative products and services company which was founded in 2003. I've been a professional artist for over 25 years, and I want to leverage every experience I've had in my education and career to help artists discover their strengths, thrive in their creative journey, avoid pitfalls, and use their gifts to make the world a better place.

Many artists are fuzzy about their specific calling as an artist, feel stuck or confused, want to take their skills to another level, wonder if they were built for something more. Often artists just need some advice and direction from a trusted voice to figure out which way to go with their creative career.

There are hundreds of ways to make a living as an artist, so it's more important than ever that creatives figure out exactly what they were built to accomplish. Artists need to discover their identity, calling, and core marketable strengths. Once those attributes are determined, artists should set goals, plan their work, then work their plan.

You were born at a great time. In many ways, we are in a modern day Renaissance for creatives. There are significant cultural, economic, and technological factors that have converged in this generation (which I'll explain in later chapters) that provide an opportunity for you like no other time in history. With all of the new-found opportunities for artists, coupled with creative industry reports predicting continued growth (cited in chapter 11), it's more important than ever for creatives to clearly identify their creative identity and calling.

I am determined to encourage as many artists as possible with this book because I believe it will change the trajectory of their career. Even one small pivot now, will make a huge difference later. More importantly, I believe it will provide artists with a sense of purpose, passion, and motivation like they have never experienced before.

So who would benefit from reading this book? The short answer is every artist and creative. As artists, we need encouragement and motivation to identify our artistic voice, develop our talents and skills, seek out opportunities to learn from other artists, establish creative and career goals, learn how to use our gifts to help others, and develop action plans that light a fire under our artistic posteriors.

I have identified 5 key seasons in an artist's life where wisdom and direction are critical. Throughout this book I refer to artists in these seasons as the "S5 Audience". Even though college counselors assist students by providing resources to help them prepare for and obtain employment, most are not equipped to help creative students find their calling and core strengths.

My undergraduate experience consisted of a schedule of required courses that were designed to encourage exploration of different mediums and approaches, but I didn't have a single class, professor, assignment, or passing comment designed to figure out what my core creative strengths were, let alone what my creative identity or calling was. There was no discussion or emphasis at any point about taking a look at our hard-wiring or life experiences as clues to where we might thrive the most.

I don't blame colleges. They are (for the most part) for-profit entities that must enroll enough students to keep the doors open and they can't hold the hand of every student. However, I fear we may have overlooked an important aspect of creative learning.

There was a time when many believed that your occupation was just as much a calling as it was a means to make a living. There used to be a built in process for mentoring. Prior to and during the Renaissance, there were apprenticeships, journeyman, and master craftsmen. This is still alive in some creative professions but is largely absent in most.

There are also few resources available to help people transition into the creative field from other fields, or to help struggling creatives find their way again. With increased opportunities comes increased complexity which can lead to a lack of clarity for artists attempting to determine which creative career to pursue.

My goal in writing this book is to provide a resource that enables creative to identify their calling and plan their education and careers based on their core marketable strengths, all while living a fulfilling life and making the world a better place. S5 Represents the five key seasons a person in the creative industry needs to intersect with a mentor, coach, or someone with more experience to point them in the right direction.

There are various conferences and events that foster an environment for mentoring artists. I work primarily in the animation industry and attend a conference called the Creative Talent Network Animation Expo in Burbank, California each November.

This conference is still a fairly small venue (relative to other large conferences such as Comic-Con) and the entire focus revolves around mentoring, sharing, and artistic growth. Once you determine your creative industry and potential career track, I highly recommend researching some conferences and events to attend in order to learn, grow, and network.

S5 Seasons

Here's a description of each of the S5 seasons/categories. Pinpoint which one you belong to and keep that in mind as you read this book.

1. SENIORS (High School)

Choosing a creative career track begins with the college or post-high school training a senior picks. My goal is to get great resources into the hands of high-school seniors, school career counselors, and high-school art teachers.

2. SOPHOMORES (College)

College Sophomores have a critical window of opportunity to declare a major, switch majors, or even switch schools. Many sophomores realize they are in the wrong track, but they are afraid to pivot because they have

2 years invested. Nothing could be worse than going 2 more years down the wrong creative track when they sense a change is really needed.

I want to provide advice, and get information and resources into the hands, heads, and hearts of college sophomores which will empower them to make sure they are being educated according to their core strengths, passion, and calling.

3. STARTING OUT

I know first hand that college training, though crucial to gaining employment, is only half of the education necessary for a thriving career. Beginning a creative career and working "hands on" in the industry is the other half of the educational equation. I want to help prepare creatives for real world experience, track down internships, help them develop relational skills and work habits that set them apart from the crowd, and find ways to get a foot in the door of their dream job! This is also a critical time to decide if the student should pursue a graduate degree.

4. STARTING OVER

After 13 years in a graphic design and illustration career, I found myself discontent and, eventually quit my job to open an animation company. I've seen many people take the courageous step to transition into a creative field that better fits their passions and core strengths, or even transition from an unrelated career to one in the creative arts.

For example, one of our TimbuktoonCloud team members flew helicopters for the military for 12 years, then decided to pursue her dream of working in the animation industry! Another great friend and long time Timbuktoons leadership level employee actually went to Seminary and planned on working in a church, until he felt called back into the creative arts. For over 13 years he has thrived while using his talents for meaningful projects for churches, companies, and non-profits. The thought of starting over can be scary and overwhelming so I want to help creatives who are making, or thinking of making, that transition.

5. STRUGGLING

Creatives are often multi-talented. They may jump from one creative passion to another. Many artists often doubt their capability and have a hard time seeing their best creative strengths. Almost every creative I know gets to a point of frustration and confusion some time in their career. They get stuck and need guidance and trusted input from a mentor. I want to help this group of creatives gain an understanding of their calling and core marketable strengths. Furthermore, I hope to help equip them with a practical real-world game plan to help them thrive again.

I wish I had a creative mentor or coach intersect my life at one of these critical five seasons of life. I've enjoyed my journey, but I really think I would have benefited from some key advice during each of those seasons.

If you wish to discover a sense of clarity, purpose, and passion, and if you want to develop a practical game plan on how to move forward with motivation and intentionality, then I believe this book will help you tremendously in the season you find yourself in now.

What Is This Book About?

This is a book about purpose. It is a book about dreams. It is a book about learning specifically why you are here and how to thrive as an artist. There is only one you. You have a purpose and a specific creative calling.

Creatives are a unique sort. We are often type cast the same, but we are really quite different from each other. The common thread we share is that we are usually multi-talented creatives, completely or somewhat confused as to what our specific calling is and sense we are on a creative journey to discover our purpose. If that resonates with you then you have stumbled upon the right book.

My creative career has seen success but I've experienced a fair share of failure, false starts, and frustrating dead ends in my creative education and career. I have learned as much, or more, from my failures and struggles as I have my successes. I want you to connect to this book no matter what educational or career stage you find yourself in, and I want you to be encouraged and empowered to take the next small step in the right direction.

I love this verse from the Bible. Zechariah 4:10a says, "Do not despise these small beginnings, for the LORD rejoices to see the work begin" We often think we need to "go big or go home", but great things all start with small beginnings.

Michael Jordan had a first dunk. John Lassiter animated a first character. Tom Hanks had a first audition. Jake Shimabukuro strummed and plucked his first ukulele. Pablo Picasso drew his first figure drawing. Jerry Seinfeld wrote a first joke. Rembrandt rendered a first attempt at chiaroscuro. Shakespeare wrote a first play. Mozart hummed a first tune. Bruce Lee threw a first kick. Martin Luther King Jr. had a first speech.

After reading this book, you will be ready to take the next single step toward a thriving creative career. If you pivot your thinking by small degrees now, the choices you make will impact your career and your life profoundly in years to come. Do not despise small beginnings. All great masters began this way!

CREATIVITY DEFINED

In conversations I have with people, when I tell them what I do, a typical response I get goes something like this. They say something along the lines of, "I can't draw a stick figure." or "I don't have a creative bone in my body."

I disagree. Everyone is creative, just in different ways. To create is human. We are creative beings by design. It's one of the things that separates us from animals.

If you stumbled upon this book and you are not in a typical creative career field, it's no accident. You are a creative too. You just use a different tool set. Think about what you do creatively and apply the principles in this book. You may discover a hidden calling that you were unaware of. I've heard people from many "non-creative" careers state that what they do is "1/2 science, and ½ art". What they typically mean is that they are trained on the facts, but to implement what they know, there is also a gut feel or a creative nuance that comes into play.

My wife is a middle-school language arts teacher. Most wouldn't consider that a creative field necessarily, but I'm often amazed at the creative ways she interacts with kids, searches out the underdog, uses out-of-the-box thinking and creative resources. She takes what could be a boring topic for many middle school students and, thru relationship building and creativity, makes it relevant, engaging, and even entertaining. For example, she recently used Sokka's Haiku Rap Battle clip (from Nickelodeon's series, *Avatar: The Last Airbender*) in a lesson about poetry. Her kids loved it and will never forget what Haiku is. More importantly they enjoyed learning in a creative way.

I've seen a construction foreman creatively solve a construction hiccup. I've seen dentists and doctors use creativity to establish their practices and create spaces that make patients feel at ease. I've seen missionaries in the Dominican Republic use creativity to build relationships, mentor and employ young men, bring clean water to refugee camps, and coordinate multiple teams of volunteers.

All three of my children play travel soccer and would stay on the field all day every day if they could. Recently my oldest son went to an overnight soccer camp for four days at Clemson University. In addition to coaching, drills, and conditioning, there were two types of tournament play spanning the four days. Each player was on a regular 11v11 team, but they were also on a 6v6 barefoot futsal team.

The 11v11 tournament was for developing team strategy, learning nuances of their positions, and an overall understanding of the game. What was the main purpose of the futsal focus? Creativity! Yes, even sports require creativity! New moves are developed and made famous by sports stars, but they all started with creative sports play! Creativity is essential in every career field.

You are innately creative. Don't think for a second that you lack creative gifts to be used to serve others. My job here is to take you through a process from ambiguity to action. I developed a format for this book called *the D5 Funnel* to help artists do just that.

Each section is designed to move you closer to clarity and closer to concrete practical action. Just as a funnel collects a broad and somewhat random flow of a substance and draws it into a singular point of action, in a similar fashion this book is designed to move you from vagueness or uncertainty, to focused concrete action toward specific goals.

THE D5 FUNNEL *(Your Creative Roadmap)*

1. **Developing Trust**

2. **Describing the Landscape**

3. **Discovering Your Creative Calling**

4. **Developing Your Plan**

5. **Doing the Work**

In the first section, I will attempt to DEVELOP trust because you deserve a credible voice. In the second section, I'll DESCRIBE the current landscape highlighting opportunities and challenges. The third section is designed to help you DISCOVER your creative calling. The fourth section gets very practical and will help you DEVELOP your specific creative road map. Finally the fifth section is where the rubber meets the road and you begin to DO the work.

If you are serious about using this book as a development tool, I highly recommend you get a sketchbook or a spiral notebook to journal and take notes as you read. There will also be a few specific exercises where a journal will be required to write down specific discovery results.

DEVELOPING TRUST

Whoever is careless with the truth in small matters cannot be trusted with important matters.

Albert Einstein

My goal with this chapter is less about sharing my story and more about developing trust. I know that the rest of this book will be more impactful if you trust the source. I can't answer all of your questions but I'll do my best to share anything that I think may help you in some way. To borrow a phrase from pastor, author, and leadership expert Andy Stanley, "I can't fill your cup, but my job is to empty mine."

I've had some wins but I have also failed at times and I've learned that failure is key to growth. Failure due to laziness or unethical behavior is stupid, but failure due to taking risks and attempting great things is both healthy and necessary for growth. The beautiful thing about failing is that you learn from each step and it means you are moving with intentionality.

I mention struggle and failure because I don't want you to read this book thinking I'm any different than you. I hope you can relate to my experiences and I pray that I might become a trusted voice.

CHAPTER 1

My Story

Do what you can, with what you have, where you are.
Theodore Roosevelt

Honesty and transparency make you vulnerable.
Be honest and transparent anyway.
Mother Theresa

It was a sunny day in Washington, DC. I had on my only dress shirt and pair of slacks. It was my first real corporate interview. It was a far cry from any other type of job I held - especially when contrasted with the hospital cafeteria where I had been working during my first 2 years of college. I wasn't too nervous (ignorance is bliss) and felt like I was just taking the next logical step which wasn't well planned or intentional. It was simply an opportunity. I was interviewing for a graphic arts intern position, but I knew very little about the agency.

Fast forward 13 years. I had climbed the ranks and became the Operations Manager of the Visual Communications Branch (which offered graphic design, printing, and photography services) and was leading a team of 18 people for the Department of the Interior. I had reached the pinnacle of that specific career track and I found myself there by taking the next logical step. One opportunity led to another. I'd walk through the door. Work hard. Walk through another door.

Sounds like a great story right? It was, except 13 years into it I finally started thinking about what I really wanted to do when I grew up. I started asking questions. What do I want to do with my life? What dreams did I have as a kid? Why didn't I pursue them? I also found myself doing less creative work, and more people managing. I worked long hours and had a long commute. My creativity stifled and I felt like a caged animal. I was at the peak of my career - and I hated it.

My wife and I had two small children by then and we purchased several Pixar and VeggieTales videos (circa 2002-2003). I had never considered a career in animation but began watching special features on the DVDs and researching everything I could find about these companies and the animation process. I gained a new found realization that animation was a masterful art form and I was also reminded of how much animated films and great stories impacted my childhood.

The logistics and likelihood of working at Pixar or Disney for me at that time were about the same as scratching a winning lottery ticket while simultaneously being struck by lightning. I had played with some early 3d (now better known as CG) animation programs but found them stifling. I looked into going back to school for animation but didn't have the budget or the time with the responsibilities and joys of a growing family.

The three things that were my saving grace were a book, a DVD, and a software program. The book was "The Art of Monsters Inc.". The DVD was a VeggieTales DVD that had special features showing concept art. The program was Macromedia Flash.

The one-two-punch combo of the book and the DVD opened up a new world for me as I realized I was more suited as a vis dev (visual development) artist than an animator, especially if I were to work at a CG studio.

I had also been playing around with two new interactive software applications to create animated transitions, buttons, and presentations. They were Macromedia Director, and Macromedia Flash. Director was too complex and the learning curve too steep for my patience, but Flash was more intuitive once you understood key frames and tweening.

This program would, of course, eventually be purchased by growing software giant Adobe and although designed as a web development tool, Flash would unexpectedly be put into use as a broadcast animation tool (and is still one of the top 2D animation software packages used for television animation).

So, that was it. I would learn how to produce character animation with Flash; however I would focus most of my development in the vis dev arena. Since I had an illustration background, this plan just seemed to click. I loved what Big Idea was doing and what they stood for so my plan was to build up a vis dev portfolio and some short Flash animations (which were horrible when I think back to them now) and I would one day apply for a job at Big Idea.

As a surprise, my wife (who knew I was thinking and praying about this) called Big Idea to ask for a tour. The problem was, we lived in Maryland and Big Idea was in Lombard, Illinois at the time. The kind receptionist informed my wife that they didn't really give tours. During the conversation my wife mentioned that we were from Maryland. The receptionist said, "Wow. Maryland? And you want to come all the way here for a tour?"

As fate would have it, she said this right as one of Big Idea's artists, who happened to be from Maryland himself, was walking by her desk. This kind young artist got on the phone with my wife, said he'd love to give us a tour if we came to town. The next thing I knew we purchased plane tickets for the family and made plans to head to Lombard, Illinois.

Our fellow Marylander gave me a three hour tour (insert *Gilligan's Island* music here) while my wife graciously wrangled our curious and active toddlers. After the tour, I knew I wanted a career in the animation field.

In addition to the tour I had an opportunity to have my portfolio reviewed by a lead visual development artist who was there at the time. Little did I know they were about to lay every one off due to some financial struggles and a legal battle. (It's an amazing story. You can read all about it in the book *Me, Myself, and Bob* by Phil Vischer found in the resources section at the end of the book.)

I would have loved to apply to work at BigIdea and was disappointed they were going thru such struggles. But at this point I knew for sure that the next phase of my career would be in the world of animation. As a result, I researched local animation schools and visited one in Alexandria, VA, but I just couldn't fit it into my schedule since I had a demanding job, long commute to DC every day, and a young family at home.

Somewhere during that season, it also occurred to me that I was essentially running a business for Uncle Sam. Our unit worked on a full cost recovery basis. This meant that our branch was funded by the federal government but we had to compete with the private sector, charge for our services, and it meant that we had to at least break even each year – fully recovering our costs. After 18 months of successfully managing this branch and recovering our costs, I realized that I had what was needed to run a business and this helped me see new possibilities. (See how one season prepares you for the next?)

A few months later, I read a little known book at the time titled *The Purpose Driven Life*, by Rick Warren (also available in the resources section of this book). I was at a place where I needed clarity and purpose. This book intersected my life at the perfect time and pushed me to do something a little crazy.

I found myself at a crossroads. At 33, five months into our first single-family home with a wife and two toddlers, I quit my job, emptied out my 401k, took one of the largest steps of faith in my life, and started an animation and graphic design company (with my wife's full support and tremendous encouragement).

The purpose of that story in the context of this book is to lead us to a key question. What if an experienced mentor with a broad knowledge of the visual arts intersected my life the day of my first interview, or better yet, early in my senior year of high school? What if a trusted friend who had knowledge about the arts were to point me to my calling and encourage me to define and pursue my career dreams even if they seemed out of reach or completely ridiculous? I may have been 13 years further down the road in a specific career track that was in the center of my calling.

I want this book to serve that purpose for you. I want to push you to drill down to your core and clearly define who you are and why you are here. I want to help you arrive at your moment of clarity now and encourage you to take bold steps to pursue your calling.

CHAPTER 2

Tuition and Dues

Failure is the opportunity to begin again more intelligently.

Henry Ford

Failures are finger posts on the road to achievement.

C. S. Lewis

Transparency, Failure, and Perseverance

I shared my credentials in the previous chapter only because they provide credibility. Experience and education help lend weight to your words and help provide confidence that you know what you are talking about. However, there is another teacher I have had which has taught me just as much, if not more, than success and a range of experience in the creative arts. Failure.

Read the honest biography of any great person of history and you'll find failure and struggle as key cast members. I don't say this to incite fear or cause discouragement. I'm merely being authentic in an attempt to help readers embrace this part of the journey as necessary and even positive. Don't get me wrong. I'm not a narcissist or suggesting we look for ways to fail. They will come on their own so let's be ready and leverage them to our benefit. Following are a few examples.

In the first year of my business (2003-2004), I had 3000 of our first animated DVD product replicated, took 1000 them to a large conference and sold (drum roll please) 17. It took years to sell all of those DVDs but through that struggle I learned how to executive produce, market, and (eventually) sell an independent animated product. Before moving to a studio in GA (where I finally had storage space) I had about 20 boxes of the DVDs in my office with a piece of paper taped to the front which read, "Tuition and Dues". It was a reminder to me that this wasn't a failure, but an education.

At Timbuktoons, we have faced at least two major economic downturns (2009 and 2013) which resulted in having to make major changes and lay off great friends. Each experience was painful, however I wouldn't trade those seasons because of what they taught me. In each instance of failure, I can trace a path to future success. For the entrepreneur and the artist failure is often the seed of future success. In order for it to germinate however, it must be fertilized with optimism, and watered with perseverance. Otherwise, you may throw in the towel when things get tough.

The point I'm making here is that struggle and failure are an integral part of the journey. They help make us who we are. If you have seen the *Lord of the Rings* trilogy, you'll recall a scene where Frodo and Sam are walking along during an uneventful leg of their journey, and they begin discussing the heroes and legends of old. They wonder aloud if others will be reading about them in a book some day.

I think we are much like these Hobbits. We are full of imperfections and quirks. We walk along our journey, facing and overcoming challenges, all the while wondering if we'll be remembered for our contribution. At some point in the journey, we realize the struggles and how we respond to them are what impacts our legacy. I don't say that in an egotistical way, but at some point, perseverance gives way to confidence and a quiet strength. We see then that failures were our friends.

You've probably heard this analogy before, but it's worth repeating. During metamorphosis, a caterpillar becomes a butterfly (or a moth) and struggles it's way out of the cocoon (or chrysalis) and flies away. If anyone attempts to "help" by breaking the cocoon or chrysalis open, the creature will be unable to fly. During the struggle to squeeze out of the cocoon or chrysalis, vital fluids necessary for flight are pushed into the outer regions of the wings enabling flight. The struggle they experience is essential to their ability to fly.

Now that you have views both my highlight reel (bio and accomplishments) along with some of my behind-the-scenes footage (failures and struggles), I hope I have gained a level of trust. My prayer is that when you read the following pages it will be akin to hearing advice from a good friend who has your best interest at heart and wants to point you to a better place.

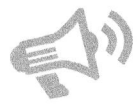

DESCRIBING THE LANDSCAPE

A pessimist sees the difficulty in every opportunity; an optimist sees the opportunity in every difficulty.

Winston Churchill

If we were to draw up a list right now of pros and cons for artists, I believe the pros would far outweigh the cons, especially for an artist with not only talent, but work ethic, relational skills, optimism, perseverance, and a little bit of courage. Before we take a look at our current landscape, let's go back a few years to a time when artists thrived.

CHAPTER 3

The Renaissance

Where the spirit does not work with the hand, there is no art.

Leonardo da Vinci

My wife and I recently rented and watched "The Monuments Men". It's a low budget, but great film about an unlikely World War II platoon tasked to rescue artistic masterpieces from Nazi thieves and return them to their owners.

I loved this film because not only is it based on a true story, but it highlights the reasons why art is so important in terms of history and culture. Appreciating beauty and art, and exhibiting creativity are a few of the key things that make us human and display the fingerprint of a creator. The Monuments Men saved works of art from several key time periods including a period known as the Renaissance.

The period of history known as the Renaissance, which began in 14th century Italy and expanded throughout Europe into the 1700's, was a historical game-changer for many aspects of culture, but especially for the arts. Renaissance essentially means "Rebirth". This period spawned a continent wide resurgence and appreciation for the arts. The net effect of this seismic shift allowed creatives to pursue various forms of art as a career and a calling.

When I was in college, one of the most memorable courses I took was "The History of the Renaissance and the Reformation", I remember our professor pointing out that if Leonardo Da Vinci, Michelangelo, Donotello, or Raphael would have been born a generation earlier, they would have been farmers or blacksmiths (and the Teenage Mutant Ninja Turtles would have had names like Bob, Al, Fred, and Tom). Both incredibly noble professions, but these artists talent would never have seen the light of day.

During the Renaissance however, several cultural, economic, and technological shifts coincided providing optimal conditions for artists to thrive. It was an unprecedented time, often referred to whenever an industry experiences a time of resurgence and prosperity.

CHAPTER 4

The New Rennaissance

*For last year's words belong to last year's language and
next year's words await another voice.*

T.S. Eliot

You and I were born at a great time in history. In many ways, we are in a modern day Renaissance for creatives. There are significant cultural, economic, and technological factors that have converged in this generation which provide an opportunity for us unlike any other time period.

Many creative industries are thriving and continue to grow. For example, the animation industry is expected to continue experiencing steady growth thru 2016 and beyond due to the proliferation of second screen devices, games, apps, and other cultural factors. *(Source: Global Animation Industry Report 2014, ResearchAndMarkets.com)*

The global animation industry in 2013 was $222 Billion. Major markets include the US, Canada, Japan, China, France, Britain, Korea and Germany. The growth rate is 7%. The animation industry remains one of the fastest growing industries. Animation is popular in every demographic and the proliferation of alternate ways of viewing content and the ability to target niche markets are contributors to growth.

Major companies such as Apple, Google, Starbucks, Disney/Pixar, Amazon, and the like, value creativity at every level in their culture and output, and the commercial success of these entities has garnered the attention of the world. Big industry used to value the cog in the wheel, performing a singular function with no thought of, or room for, applying creativity or individual thought. However, in today's business world, most major industries foster and reward creativity.

Think about how many things we use every day that required creativity at some level. Whether it's the chair you are sitting in, the computer or tablet you are reading this on, the music you are listening to, the design of the cup you are drinking coffee from, or the flavor of the coffee you are drinking, someone applied creativity to concept, develop, and produce it!

CHAPTER 5

Art and Technology

*The art challenges the technology, and
the technology inspires the art.*

John Lasseter

In addition to the new found respect for creativity, there are also technological reasons why this is a great time to be a creative. Technology and art are inherently connected. They always have been. Art needs a medium. Mediums present themselves thru current technology. From textiles to print making; from forging metal to producing CG films; art and technology are always connected.

When I first began working as an intern at the agency I mentioned previously, I learned graphic design techniques using a large stat camera, a very basic (and very expensive) digital layout computer called a Kodak KEEPS system, layout board, a hot wax machine used to adhere artwork to the layout board, hand drawn registration and crop marks, acetate and masking film overlays when design for multiple print colors was necessary.

Then we got Pagemaker! Then QuarkXpress! Then Illustrator and Photoshop! I was watching the digital print revolution take place right before my eyes in a matter of just a few short years.

The same thing was happening in the entertainment industry with all of the technology and software that came out of Lucas Film and Pixar's development success. Non-linear or digital editing, compositing, and digital sound design, along with both digital 2D and CG animation, combined to completely change the industry landscape as we knew it.

Chances are that the digital revolution took place before you were born or before you were aware of such things, but the digital revolution and the internet are your best friends.

Never before have artists had such affordable and powerful hardware and software available to them.

Never before have artists had access to so much electronic communication and file transferrability as we do today.

Never before has there been such a widespread opportunity for creatives in so many fields and industries.

Never before have there been so many schools and universities that value the arts and offer such a plethora of creative degrees.

CHAPTER 6

A Caution

If opportunity doesn't knock, build a door.

Milton Berle

With every shift of this magnitude, there are bound to be some negative effects as well. One negative effect that I've seen and that I'm very concerned about is the number of artists graduating from art schools with a degree, but with no sense of calling and no clear plan forward. Many students are graduating with all the necessary requirements but with no real understanding of specialization or the importance of having concrete career goals.

Another concern I have is the number of students graduating with little career placement and assistance and to few creative jobs to sustain them. LA, NY, Atlanta, Nashville, and other cities are attracting many college graduates. However it can be extremely difficult to break into the creative industries of those cities as a recent graduate due to the sheer number of artists moving to those creative hubs.

If you are reading this book and are a recent or soon to be Graduate, I'm so glad you bumped into this book at this time. I think you have a great opportunity because of these factors as more small studios continue to open in cities (and countries) that aren't traditionally seen as creative hubs.

There's a way that you can apply your self in order to separate from the pack. I've seen hundreds of applications and demo reels come across my desk and the ones that stand out have these qualities.

Actual Talent

I hate to say it, but some students should have been told up front during their college application (or long before) that they should focus on a different career track. Let me balance that by saying, none of us are as good as we would like to be and with the exception of a small handful of people on earth, there will always be someone more talented than you or me.

What I'm highlighting here is the fact that there are hobbyists who think art is fun but really, truly, do not have a gift in this area. I believe everyone has a gift to use, but it's critical to discover what that gift is before spending thousands of dollars on a two or four year degree just because art is fun.

Work Ethic

At Timbuktoons, we have had a few interns and TimbuktoonCloud Team members (offsite freelancers) who applied with an amazing portfolio but unfortunately displayed a poor work ethic. They did a wonderful job selecting the right pieces for their portfolio, but their work never matched their portfolio, and they would rarely deliver a project in on time.

People Skills

At Timbuktoons, we have also had a few people come thru our virtual and/or brick-and-mortar doors with amazing talent, but very poor people skills. Creative environments are fun, but artists must remember and display that they are professionals. We need to take an honest look at how we work with others and make adjustments if necessary.

The fact is, most studios would rather hire someone with lesser talent but over-the-top work ethic and people skills, than someone with an insane amount of talent who couldn't hit a due date.

Over the years, I have witnessed sports teams hire an athlete with superstar talent even though the athlete had a history of problems with discipline, work ethic, or relational fallout. I can't think of a single case where anything good came out of the decision. Even if a successful season occurred it was short lived and left a wake of damaged team moral and unhealthy team culture. The same principles apply in a studio or career.

If you continually hone your craft, under-promise, over-deliver, work well with others, and never miss a deadline, your perseverance and hard work will pay off with success.

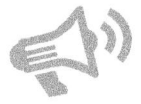

DISCOVERING YOUR CREATIVE CALLING

The mystery of human existence lies not in just staying alive,
but in finding something to live for.

Fyodor Dostoyevsky, *The Brothers Karamazov*

Distilled to it's baseline ingredients, your life's purpose is largely found from three things; identity, calling, and experience. Part discovery, part journey; all hard work and an exciting ride if you are up for the challenge. Let's dive in!

CHAPTER 7

Identity Defined

You can train monsters like this all you want,
but you can't change who they are!
James P. Sullivan, *from the film Monsters University*

The Merriam-Webster dictionary defines identity as:

The distinguishing character or personality of an individual.

If you are like me, chances are you haven't ever really thought much about this early in your career. Most of us don't until we face a crisis, major transition, or are facing some type of decision that will impact our lives in a significant way.

For some people their sense of identity is wrapped up in their career, for some it's wrapped up in being a parent, or a soldier, or an artist, etc. But identity really goes much deeper than that.

Identity has to do with who you are at the core level as a uniquely designed individual. You are a one-of-a-kind masterpiece with hardwiring and experiences that no one else has.

Occupations, roles, seasons, and situations change, but your identity remains constant.

I find that abstract concepts are better explained by specific examples. Since I'm an animation nerd, I thought I'd use an example from an animated movie.

Learn a lesson from Mike Wazowski from *Monsters University*. (Forget what you know about him from *Monsters Inc.* for a moment.) His whole identity was wrapped up in becoming a scarer. It's all he thought about since childhood. His story arc (and Sulley's as well) in the film is really about finding his identity.

This example is relevant for you and I. If you identified with any of the S5 categories I mentioned early in the book, I think you will be able to relate to Mike.

You have dreamed of becoming a certain type of creative, but you're not 100% sure if that is your true identity or not. Interest and desire do not equal identity. Identity is only found in the journey and is usually different than what it appears to be on the surface.

At a critical moment in the film, after several suprise wins in a fraternity competition, Sully realizes that they have won through a combination of luck and hard work.

He comes to understand that their team does not have what it takes to win the final challenge. He turns to Mike and says, "You can train monsters like this all you want, but you can't change who they are!"

Even the initials of the fraternity they belonged to pointed to how they were perceived by others and how they really felt about themselves. Oozma Kappa (OK). Their motto was "We're OK!" That was their identity. We're just OK. Nothing special. No real talent to share here.

Later in the film, after coming to grips with the fact that he was not a natural scarer, Mike says to Sulley, "I thought if I wanted it enough I could show everyone that Mike Wazowski is someone special."

Mike's sense of self worth was wrapped up in his identity as a scarer. But his real identity was as a forward thinking coach. He brought out the best in others, taught them how to work as a team, and found a way to win. Infact, during one of the very last shots of the film, at the end of a montage of scenes showing how Mike and Sulley climbed the ranks from the mail room to the scare floor, just as they are about to step foot on the scare floor as official scarers, Sully looks at Mike and says, "Are you ready, coach?"

You'll miss the line if you're not paying close attention, but it punctuates Mike's mature acceptance and celebration of his true identity.

All along he was bringing out the best in everyone around him. All along he was studying every angle of scaring. All along he was finding a way to win. But it took a journey of self discovery to understand his true identity.

This was Sulley's arc too. His identity was wrapped up in his family name. His family had been top scarers for generations. Sulley was a shoo-in and clearly had raw talent as a scarer. He seemed to take nothing seriously and expected everything to fall into place for him. Mike and Sulley were polar opposites.

At the climax of the film, just after an extremely vulnerable scene where Sulley confesses to Mike that although he acts brave and carefree he is actually terrified and confused, the two hatch a plan to scare adult police officers (an impossible feat by monster standards) to generate enough scream power to get back home.

Overwhelmed by this task, Sulley blurts out, "Mike I can't do this!" To which Mike quickly replies, "Stop being a Sullivan and start being you!" Almost instantly, Sulley's resolve returns but with a new found sense of identity and the two scare their way back home. Mike coached Sulley's identity out of him and both characters learned their identity through a crisis and a journey. We discover our identities through experience, struggle and intentional seeking.

A few scenes later Sulley tracks down Mike who's leaving the campus (both having been kicked out of school) and greets him with a pep talk that demonstrates he has finally grasped who they both are. Seeing Mike's identity struggle more clearly, Sully says, "And you just think you're Ok? Mike, you're not scary, but you are fearless!" In this one statement, Sully points to Mike's identity in it's most distilled and primal form – fearless.

What about you? Have you lived enough life, been through enough struggle, intentionally searched your soul, sought enough council, prayed deep enough prayers, to understand, embrace, and celebrate your true identity?

About a year and a half ago, I was at a season of life where I needed clarity and wanted to make sure (to the best of my ability) that I was doing the work I was supposed to do. I wanted to make sure the rest of my life had maximum impact and meaning. I went thru a six week process of intentional discovery to nail down my identity and my calling; two different, but related things.

After sifting thru several markers I came to rest on an identity statement: *I am a creative, God-seeking encourager.*

Simple words. Profound meaning. It was really what went into nailing down these few words that mattered.

I am "a" creative (a noun, not an adverb)**:** I've always had a creative visual arts bent.

God-seeking: I look for God in stuff. This isn't a Christian book, but I am a Christian at my core. There's something in me that always looks for God's finger prints.

Encourager: From my personality type, to my relationships, to my vocation. I thrive most when I'm spurring others on to good things; when I can say or do something that makes them want to take another step or move to a better place or have courage to face uncertainty. I'm writing this book out of my identity.

To give another example using our Monsters University discussion above, I would describe Mike Wazowski's identity as: *a fearless and unconventional, motivational catalyst.*

Notice he had an idea about his identity but was slightly off track until life forced him to discover and accept his real identity.

Discovering your identity takes intentionality and dedicated time. If you're stuck or unclear, it may take a coach or mentor to help you to ask the right questions. It's a process, not a formula. It's a journey, not a recipe. But my hope is that this section will help you begin to process and discover your identity.

CHAPTER 8

Identity Markers

*Every child is an artist. The problem is how to remain
an artist once we grow up.*

Pablo Picasso

It would be great if we could condense years of experience and key events into a few paragraphs to discover our identity. It's one thing to unpack the identity of a fictitious cinematic, or literary character, but an altogether different task to define our own. The good thing is there are several things you can assess to help discover your identity. Let's look at a few.

1. Personality Type

Are you an introvert or extrovert? Do you like risk, or does it scare you to death? Are you a broad brush visionary or do you prefer working out the details? You absolutely must understand as much as you can about your personality type.

Some of this only comes with life experience but there are some very accurate tests you can take including the Myers-Briggs, or the DISC Assessment Test. Personally I prefer the DISC Assessment Test. There are great resources to help you see what career roles may fit you best, based on your personality type.

2. Childhood Interests and Background

What did you dream about doing as a child when there were no obstacles to thinking big? What came naturally to you? What held your interest so long you forgot about time? What talent do you have that others have affirmed? What did you read, see, or hear that gave you a sense of awe and wonder?

I believe those are all clues to your purpose. I have 2 step-brothers, one of whom is very close in age to me so growing up we played a lot together. When we were kids, I would get lost drawing characters, creatures, and space ships while my step-brother would get lost playing in the dirt with Hot Wheels and Matchbox Cars. Today I draw and produce animation for a living and my step-brother operates multi-million dollar construction cranes with cockpits that rival the space shuttle.

3. Passions

What makes you come to life? What excites and ignites you? What bothers you and keeps you up at night? What is broken in the world that you would like to help fix?

4. Family and Friend's Assessment

Spend some time talking with those closest to you to get their perspective on your identity. If you haven't yet downloaded the "GET CLEAR. GET GOING. 5 Days to Creative Career Clarity Workbook", please sign up for my newsletter (toddhampson.com) and it will be sent to you within an hour. In it, there are specific exercises with questions for you to ask family and friends. Outside input helps to confirm and clarify our own assessment, and often opens our eyes to other things we had not previously considered.

5. Worldview

We each have a belief system. Even those who claim to have no belief system have a belief system. Even those who have never consciously thought about their worldview have one. It's impossible to get away from. It's important to define and understand the core principles of your belief system or worldview. It consciously and unconsciously informs your thought process, decisions and aspirations. Your worldview most definitely impacts your perspective regarding identity and calling or purpose.

6. Most Unique Attributes.

What odd combinations reside within you? What makes you unique? Many times the seemingly contradictory combinations of skills and interests we have are clues to our specific purpose.

Using an example from the Bible, king David was a warrior and a harpist. What?! He proved himself in battle over and over again, but he also played the harp for king Saul.

In the story of his life both skills were used to position him and reveal his calling and purpose. Later in scripture (Acts 13:36a) it even says "David had served God's purpose in his own generation" Take a close look at your random interests. You may be surprised to find that those are the very clues that help lead you to your identity.

7. Fears

What fears do you have? They may be blocking you from discovering your true calling. When I worked with the life coach in 2013 we addressed this in depth. I listed out every fear I had, then went thru an excercise that made me list the worst possible outcome for each fear. The goal was to see what (if any) fears were blocking me from pursuing my calling.

8. Core Values

Core values become filters for finding your calling and making decisions. Spend time determining what they are. For example, my top core values are: Family, Leadership, Passion, Courage, Growth, and Selflessness. I have more, but those are the top six. If I have an opportunity or career decision to make, one of the things I do is filter the decision thru my core values. If it violates them, I don't go down that path. Over the years I've turned down work (even when my business needed the cash flow) because it didn't line up with one or more of my core values.

Your Identity Statement

Okay, remember that sketchbook or spiral notebook that I mentioned you would need? (You've been taking notes in it right?) Well, here's your first exercise.

- **Step 1:** Think thru everything you just read and write down anything you can think of for each of the numbered items above. It's well worth your time to pause here, look online, and find a reliable website to take a personality test (there are even some free versions available). I recommend the DISC Assessment Test. Also, as I mentioned above, you can receive the "GET CLEAR. GET GOING." Workbook free at <u>toddhampson.com</u> by signing up for my e-newsletter.

- **Step 2:** Write down a very loose draft version of your identity statement. Refer to my statement and the Mike Wazowski statements as examples. You want to focus on three or four key attributes that convey who you are at the core. Not who you wish you were or who you want to be, but who you are. What is innately true about you? Be very honest with yourself. It's going to be difficult to narrow it down but look for overlapping themes, words or concepts that show up over and over, and consolidate anything that can fall under a broader attribute. For example, leadership was a big theme in my identity, but it really supports and influences my role as an encourager, so my encourager attribute also encapsulates leadership. Encouragement (spurring others on to courage) requires a certain amount of leadership.

- **Step 3**: Write down three to five alternate versions of your identity statement.

- **Step 4:** Put it away for a day or two and come back to it. How does it fit now that you have had time to reflect?

- **Step 5:** Compose a final version of your identity statement.

- **Step 6:** Share it with those close to you and get their response.

- **Step 7:** Confirm or modify your statement until you know it's true. You'll reach a point where you just know that it's true of you.

Understanding and embracing your identity, core, true self, or whatever you want to call it, is essential to discovering the next key aspect of your purpose - your calling.

CHAPTER 9

Calling Defined

If God gives you something you can do,
why in God's name wouldn't you do it?

Stephen King

If identity has to do with how you are designed and equipped, calling has to do with what you are supposed to do with that knowledge. It's what you were put on earth to do. Your identity is who you are. Your calling is how you live it out daily with passion and focus.

Merriam Webster's Dictionary defines calling in two ways:

A strong desire to spend your life doing a certain kind of work (such as religious work)

The following is their second definition is what I would consider a more full and accurate version:

A strong inner impulse toward a particular course of action especially when accompanied by conviction of divine influence

Occupations, assignments, tasks, and seasons change, but your calling goes much deeper and remains constant.

Using the Mike Wazowski example, I would say that his calling or purpose is to: *bring out the best in others and pursue high performance accomplishments.*

Notice that his calling lines up with his role or assignment during The Scare Games in college, as well as his work climbing the ranks to the scare floor, then (in *Monster's Inc.*) in breaking records on the scare floor.

I have talked to people who seem to think that only people working in religious circles are called to what they do. I would argue that we are all called to do something that benefits others and I would also argue that there is no distinction between secular and sacred when it comes to your life's calling. Many creatives I've spoken with feel that their skills and passions are less legitimate than other occupations. I disagree. You are one-of-a-kind. You are here at this time in history for a reason.

In his book, <u>Me, Myself, and Bob</u>, Phil Vischer writes about how his impression of someone doing God's work was as an overseas missionary or a pastor. It was a process for him to come to understand and accept his calling as a storyteller, teacher, and media producer.

The Importance of An Outside Voice

Before I starting my company in 2003, I spent a few months that spring with a career counselor to help me prepare for the major transition. Then ten years later in the spring of 2013 I worked with a life coach (and great friend of mine) for eight weeks to further clarify my identity and calling. I didn't plan to do each of these exactly 10 years apart and both were very valuable experiences that helped me gain further clarity on the season I was about to enter.

Having an experienced outside coach's help to walk you through a process, assign homework, and draw answers out of you, is priceless. In a process like this, you will be the one to actually figure out the answers. The purpose of a coach is to have someone gently and expertly push you to do the tough soul-searching work which people don't typically make a priority. Life is busy, but what could be more valuable than dedicating a short period of time to figure out what you are supposed to do in life?

I advise artists to look for Virtual and Real-Life Mentors. Find someone in your field or in your area and ask them to mentor you. If you can't find someone in your area, check online. There are tons of blogs, training sites, podcasts, YouTube videos, books (see the Resources section), documentaries, and other outlets that allow thought leaders to virtually mentor thousands of creatives.

I have had real flesh-and-blood mentors at different seasons in life but I've also been mentored afar by leaders who don't even know me. There is no substitute for a real mentor, but be sure to capitalize on the amazing amount of resources available to you today if having a local mentor is not currently possible.

As I mentioned above, my Identity statement is: *I am a creative, God-seeking, encourager.*

Now, here's my calling statement: *My calling is to move people one step closer to their creator and their purpose.*

I found this to be true in everything I do from the relationships I build, to the work I do, to the art I create, to how and when I volunteer my time, to how I raise my children, and how I lead and love my wife.

I want to move people: I want to move their heart. I want to move their emotions. I want to move them to a better location or position.

One step closer: I don't want to be a jerk. I don't want to impose on people. I want to respect them. I want to help move people one step at a time to a better place.

Creator and purpose: I believe the more we live out who we were designed to be, the more we will thrive and find our life's purpose, and the bigger the positive impact we will have in life.

Now, let's do some work and discover your calling as an artist!

CHAPTER 10

What Is Your Creative Calling?

The only time I feel alive is when I'm painting.

Vincent Van Gogh

Discovering your calling is a tough thing to nail down and you need an intentional process. The main things needed are time and intentionality. You also need to talk to others who know you as you do this serious soul searching. That being said, I do not intend to make it more complicated than it needs to be.

Micheal Hyatt (blogger and author of <u>Platform</u>) suggests that your calling is where your passion, proficiency, and profitability align. Phil Cooke (interviewed here in a later chapter) says that the premise of his book <u>One Big Thing</u> is that your OBT is "more of a calling, a purpose - the overarching reason you're on the earth. When you figure that out, you'll find many ways to express it." So, again I want to emphasize that your calling is bigger than a job or a career, those are merely assignments or seasons.

For me, it really helped to look at all aspects of my identity and calling before writing out my statements. There was something very powerful about writing them down. It was almost like being fitted for armor. If you take this approach, be sure to bounce it off others who know you well to get confirmation.

A Personal Story To Further Illustrate

Notice that nothing in my identity or calling statements mention a job or career. It's deeper than that. We know (if you are reading this book) that one of the key avenues you'll express your calling is through your role as an artist, but what lies behind that? What drives your art? What do you create that makes you come alive? What are the drivers that make you express yourself through your art the way you do?

A few years ago I was on a mission trip and we were working in a poor city in the Dominican Republic. Children grow up in some really tough conditions.

There was one church we were working with that was strategically located to these children hope. The missionaries we work with asked me to paint a mural on a wall at the church that was visible from the street. They believed that this would attract children to this church and give them hope and help provide for their needs.

To this day, I still get choked up when I think of the hundreds of children that pass by this brightly colored mural on a run down dusty street as they see the words "Dios Es Amor". God is love.

Many of these children have not experienced love. Many have experienced abuse and neglect. But my art is a megaphone shouting to them that someone cares.

This mural that we painted builds relational bridges between a caring church and these forgotten children. That was the expression of my calling there. To move these children one step closer to their creator and their true purpose. In this case it happened to be thru my art because it's a skill that I have, but my calling is deeper and broader than my art.

Your Calling Statement

Okay, it's time to get that journal out again. We're going to use a process similar to the one we used to develop your identity statement. The difference here is, you need to focus more on how your identity is lived out. What is your purpose? What action does your calling lead you to? What keeps you up at night? What bugs you?

- **Step 1:** Make a list of common themes that show up in different areas of your life. What is the passion or the pain behind your art?

- **Step 2:** Make a list of verbs (action words) to convey how you express your passions. What action (subtle or overt) do you take to leave a mark on this world? What makes you pick up the ball and move it forward?

- **Step 3:** Create a very loose, rough draft of your calling statement.

- **Step 4:** Write down three to five alternate versions of your calling statement.

- **Step 5:** Put it away for a day or two and come back to it. How does it fit?

- **Step 6:** Compose a final version of your calling statement.

- **Step 7:** Share it with those close to you and get their response.

- **Step 8:** Confirm or modify your statement until you know it's true.

Incase You're Stuck

In the last chapter I shared how I have used outside coaching to help me prepare for a new season. You may discover that you are still stuck and may need the help of an experienced creative career coach or a life coach. I've personally found that using a trusted third party is often helpful for 4 main reasons.

1. Sometimes others see things in you that you can't.

An experienced and gifted coach can see patterns and keys that aren't as clear to you.

2. Problems can't be solved at the level where they exist.

I've found that you can't "think things clear". If you are stuck, you need an outside voice.

3. We won't typically do the hard work needed without accountability and a little healthy outside pressure.

When a coach assigns gives us homework designed to get specific results, we're more likely to be motivated to do the work which will show us real results. The added healthy pressure of being accountable to someone else is another motivating factor.

4. We will be more likely to push thru the process if we have "skin in the game".

When I hired the career coach in 2003 and the life coach in 2013, there was something extremely motivating about paying someone money to help me. For one thing, I didn't want to waste my investment. Another motivating factor was having specific cost and timeframe to complete the process. This provided instant and sustained momentum through the process. It was significant work on top of an already busy life, but knowing there was a purpose and a timeframe helped me dig deep and do the necessary work.

"GET CLEAR. GET GOING." Workbook

If you don't have time, or can't afford outside help, I would, again, highly recommend getting the (free) *GET CLEAR. GET GOING. 5 Days to Creative Career Clarity* workbook as a start. (It's free when you sign up for my e-newsletter at <u>toddhampson.com</u>). This workbook is a great first step in nailing down your identity and calling. It only takes five days to complete and it is a very practical, easy to use, and effective tool.

If you need further assistance and coaching, there are also some great books and other resources (see the resource list at the end of this book) that I recommend.

I would pause here, take some time to nail down your calling, write down you calling statement to see how it fits, then come back to this book to start developing your plan. This is important because your calling will influence your plans and goals tremendously.

I've also found that developing your plan and setting goals further clarifies your calling. If that's the case, there's nothing wrong with coming back to you calling statement to revise it a bit. The main goal is to know in your gut that it's true of you.

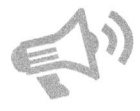

DEVELOPING YOUR PLAN

*Let our advance worrying become advance
thinking and planning.*

Winston Churchill

Hopefully by this point you've gained some clarity on your identity, calling, and general direction. Now it's time to dig a little deeper, define some specifics, and start developing a real plan.

CHAPTER 11

What Flavor Are You?

I saw the angel in the marble and carved until I set him free.
Michelangelo

This aspect of discovery is probably not as difficult or nebulous as previous things we've discussed. Chances are you know at this point if you more inclined to be a musician, or an actor, or an illustrator, or graphic designer.

There's still a bit of discovery to do here though, because most creatives are multitalented or have varying creative interests. To complicate matters, there are a multitude of niche markets and specialties within each broad creative industry or category. The goal of this chapter is to further clarify your career direction by evaluating your particular area of interest. Many people, however, have a very clear focus and there is no debate within themselves about what to pursue.

My wife knew in the 3rd grade that she was going to be a teacher. That sense of calling has never left and she is an amazing and talented educator. Even when she quit teaching to stay at home with our children when they were young, she still used her calling as a teacher and nurturer in a different role. (Remember, your calling is deeper and broader than an occupation.)

I on the other hand (as mentioned in the intro) have varying interests and talents (mostly in the visual arts) and have had different seasons focusing on different creative aspects. For me it's been more of a journey to figure it out.

What flavor are you? What broad area of interest are you most equipped to thrive within? What specific path within a particular creative industry do you need to research and pursue?

List of Creative Industries and Careers

Here are the key creative industries with a brief overview of each. For the six largest creative industries I've included some market research which includes (if available) the annual revenue, growth rate, and number of companies in that industry.

There are definitely many areas of overlap where a certain skill set or profession can be found in multiple industries but I've attempted to categorize the industries and careers as simply and as logically as possible.

I have also included some very eye-opening guest interviews that cover a few key areas. Since I operate an animation company, most of these interviews are with some great folks in the animation and entertainment industry. If your interests lie in another creative industry I'm confident that you will find their creative journeys and words of advice are applicable to any creative field.

Also, as I have mentioned previously, animation is really a culmination of all major art forms. Even some of the most niche forms of art have come into play during animation development. I have broken the list down by the major creative industry segments, and niche segments.

Lastly, I should mention that this is not an exhaustive list. There are many other careers that fall within the creative industries listed. I have attempted to include the most common careers for each industry.

THE MAJOR SEGMENTS

Animation/Interactive/Game Arts/VFX

The global animation industries revenue in 2013 was $222 Billion. Major markets include the US, Canada, Japan, China, France, Britain, Korea and Germany. The growth rate is 7%. The animation industry remains one of the fastest growing industries.

Animation is popular in every demographic and the proliferation of alternate ways of viewing content and the ability to target niche markets are contributors to growth. Animation and gaming industries are expected to have strong growth for the next several years. *(Source: Global Animation Industry Report 2014, ResearchAndMarkets.com)*

- animation writer

- story artist/storyboard artist

- visual development artist

- art director

- production designer

- character designer

- prop designer

- layout and background designer

- video editor

- motion graphics designer

- VFX modeler, rigger, animator, technical

- modeler

- sculptor

- post production artist

- technical artist/programmer

Film/Video Production

With a $90 billion annual revenue and 58,100 companies to choose from, the movie production and distribution industry has a .2% growth rate. *(Source: Global Movie Production and Distribution: Market Research Report, February 2014, IBISWorld.com)*

- short films

- commercials

- documentaries

- corporate

- feature films

Graphic Design/Communications/Marketing

With a $46 billion global revenue, and $11 billion US revenue, the graphic design/communications industry is expected to grow thru 2019 as other emerging industries require their services. *(Source: Graphic Designers in the US: Market Research Report, June 2014; Global Graphic Designers: Market Research Report, December 2013, IBISWorld.com)*

- graphic designer

- broadcast designer

- special effects artist

- web designer

- font designer

- marketing art director

- creative strategist

- brand strategist

Publishing

Global publishing has an annual revenue of $108 billion and is made up of 18,971 businesses. Growth has declined as the industry transitions to e-books and competes with self publishers and other new factors. *(Source: Global Book Publishing: Market Research Report, September 2013, IBISWorld.com)*

- writers

- editors

- business professionals

- agents

- designers

Arts Management/Business

This sector has many overlapping industries and is somewhat segmented and niche, therefore detailed and reliable research is a bit more difficult to come by.

However, some data is available such as Museums ($10bn US with 1.7% growth rate) and Licensing ($37bn US with a 2% growth rate) *(Sourcse: Museums in the US: Market Research Report, June 2014, IBISWorld.com; Intellectual Property Licensing in the US: Market Research Report, June 2014, IBISWorld.com)*

- art/print licenser

- agent

- studio owner

- art auctioneer

- art gallery owner

- art consultant

- art restorer

- museum curator

- art restorer

Performing Arts

With a $27 billion annual revenue and 766,856 companies to choose from, the performing arts industry suffered a decline during the economic downturn but is beginning to grow again. *(Source: Performers & Creative Artists in the US: Market Research Report, December 2013, IBISWorld.com)*

- costume designer

- make-up artist

- set designer

- choreographer

- actor/actress

- dance instructor

- DJ's

- Concert and event planning and design

NICHE MARKET OR COMBINED CREATIVE INDUSTRIES

Fine Arts

- sculptor

- textile artist

- painter

- ceramic artist

- printmaker

- illustrator

Artisan

- baker/culinary artist

- tattoo artist

- signmaker

- jeweler

- stained-glass artist

- mosaic artist

- hairstylist

- florist

- glassblower

- police sketch artist

Editorial Arts

- art critic

- film critic

- art historian

- book illustrator

- comic book artist

- medical illustrator

- news photographer

- arts editor

- cartoonist

- greeting card designer

- advertising designer

Professional Arts

- school art teacher

- art therapist

Engineering Design Arts

- furniture designer

- landscape designer

- architect

- interior designer

- fashion designer

- automobile designer

- product designer

- packaging designer

Musical Arts

- instrumental

- voice

- studio technician

- music producer

- record label/recording studios

Fashion and Textiles

- designer

- seamstress

- modeling

- event planning

Photography/Photo Imaging

- photographer

- photo retouching

- color correcting

- compositing

CHAPTER 12

Interviews With Some Industry Veterans

We are not cisterns made for hoarding,
we are channels made for sharing.

Billy Graham

I wanted this book to be as broad of a resource for you as I could make it. I wanted to bring in some other voices and advice from other sources prior to helping you develop your plan. So, I contacted a few of my animation and entertainment industry friends for an interview, told them about my book and how I wanted to help artists thrive, and to they all jumped right on board!

One thing I've noticed about the creative industry is that artists are generally natural sharers. They love to give back. They love to mentor and help the next generation of artists. Much like the legendary "Nine Old Men" of Disney, they willingly pass on knowledge and experience to those following behind. My heartfelt thanks goes out to each interviewee. Your contribution will be a blessing to many.

I should also note that none of the interviewees had read the manuscript of this book prior to giving the interviews and they do not necessarily adhere to, or endorse, the concepts or advice I have written in these pages. Each of their interviews is simply a stand-alone piece of content that they graciously contributed to the book to help give advice to other artists.

I should also note that I have compiled the interviews in alphabetical order, not order of perceived importance or influence. There is so much in each interview that will help every artist. I hope you will take the time to read each interview and take notes. Many times answers come in unexpected ways and I'm willing to bet that you will find unexpected answers as you read the interviews on the following pages.

Interview with: Tom Bancroft

Tom Bancroft has almost 25 years of experience in the animation industry, most of which was for Walt Disney Feature animation where he was an animator for 11 years. He has been nominated for Annie and Rueben division awards, spoken at the Kennedy Center and awarded an entry into the Chicago Children's Film Festival.

While at Disney, Bancroft had the opportunity to contribute animation on 10 animated feature films, five animated shorts, and numerous special projects and commercials. Some of the classic films include, *Beauty and the Beast, The Lion King, Aladdin, Mulan,* and *Brother Bear.* He was also a character designer and director for Big Idea Productions, makers of the family-friendly *Veggie Tales* video series.

In 2005, Bancroft had his popular art instruction book, Creating Characters with Personality published by Watson-Guptill Publishers. It has become the most recognized book on designing characters for animation, video games, comic books, and cartooning and is a required textbook at many art schools around the world. Focal Press recently published his second book, <u>Character Mentor</u> and it is already one of their best-selling art instruction books.

Bancroft co-founded Funnypages Productions, LLC and ran it for eight years. Throughout that time and continuing now, he has provided direction, art direction, illustration, character design and animation development for clients like Disney Feature films, Disney Licensing, DC comics, Marvel Licensing, Big Idea Productions, Warner Brothers, CBN, Scholastic, Lego International, DeNa Studios, and Pocketgems. He has also illustrated over 50 children's books. He also provided character art and art direction to help launch the popular kid's educational website ABCMouse.com.

Most recently Tom launched <u>Taught by a Pro</u> which has: *Online Courses for Aspiring Animators, Comic Artists, Character Designers and Illustrators*

Bancroft and his family reside in Franklin, Tennessee. You can see a gallery of some of Bancroft's work at:

http://tombancroft.designbinder.com/

http://www.imdb.com/name/nm0051642/

http://taughtbyapro.com

TODD: Tom, you're an animator, character designer, animation producer, respected industry leader, and an online business owner. Which of those roles have you enjoyed the most and why?

TOM: It's so hard to answer because I look at my career in segments. The two major pieces are the first 11 or 12 years working at studio, mostly at Disney and a couple of years at BigIdea.

Everything after that, the next 12 years, was a season of having my own company or working independently. That has really been all about character design…writing a couple books, doing contract work…and illustrating comic books, children's books, and a web comic.

The first years were in animation and I was a company guy. The second season is more independent and focused more on character design. Independent is always going to be smaller and cheaper and nothing tops my years at Disney, but they are both rewarding in different ways.

TODD: I'm sure this is tough to answer in one statement, but now that you're in a new season of your career as an artist and have had time to reflect, what's it like knowing you were part of "Disney's Renaissance" or "second golden age"?

TOM: Well, incredible. It's the thing that artistically made me. But even as a person it did in a lot of ways. I couldn't be doing what I do now, working from home as an independent in Nashville, TN. had I not had that time at Disney. I still get work daily which is directly or indirectly connected to my days at Disney.

TODD: Some have pointed out that with Lasseter and Catmull heading up Disney and the recent success of Frozen and other recent films, that it's a Disney is experiencing a "Second Renaissance", or "3rd Golden Age" for Disney. Any plans or desires to work for a studio again or are you enjoying your indie freedom?

TOM: It's probably too soon to say it's another golden age, but they have definitely had a good three or four film fun. I took my girls to see Tangled and it was only the second time I watched a CG film that I would have loved to work on. The Incredibles was the other. You could see Glen Keane's stamp on that movie (Tangled). It had so many 2d sensibilities.

That would have been a fun film to work on. So, that was one that I kind of went, ah, I wish I was back at the studio. There are days I miss the camaraderie of working and think it would be great to work at Disney, or Dreamworks, or Pixar.

TODD: What was your personal favorite Disney film or other project to work on and why?

TOM: I would have to say Mulan. I was the supervising animator for Mushu and had a lot more say in that film than any other Disney film I worked on. I have fond memories working on The Lion King and Aladdin, but Mulan for me was a completely different level because I was involved so much in preproduction. There is more work of mine in Mulan than in the seven others I touched.

TODD: Mushu is a pretty complex character too, as far as shapes, details, posing, and acting. He was such an important side-kick in the film as well. What was that pressure like?

TOM: The directors and my brother Tony all basically said, "This is a really big jump in your career. Now, not to put any pressure on you, but if they would have made Mulan in the 40's or 50's, Ward Kimball would be animating Mushu. That's the kind of level you need to hit."

Up to that point I wasn't thinking along those lines. It was a dream character that only comes along once in a while even on Disney films and I was honored to work on him.

TODD: I was clueless at the time but we went to Disney World right after they laid everyone off in Orlando. It was so sad. You could still take the tour but the place was empty. I've since watched "Dream on Silly Dreamer" which chronicles the decline and it's heart breaking.

Were you around during the Disney layoffs or did you have friends who went through that?

TOM: I worked on Brother Bear as a contractor and they wouldn't commit to hire anyone for the next film which was "A Few Good Ghosts". I moved to Franklin, TN and about three months later my buds who were still there got laid off, but I left about a year before.

TODD: What first got you interested in the animation industry?

TOM: When I was growing up, my twin brother and I thought we would be comic strip artists like Charles Shulz because we were big Peanuts fans.

We loved comic books but thought the superhero stuff was too hard to draw. Back then you didn't have any special features of behind the scenes footage. That didn't come until the advent of VCRs. So, animation wasn't on my radar.

We loved Harryhausen films though, and my brother and I did a stop motion project in junior college with a super-8 camera and some clay for a youth group thing at our church.

Then I found out that Cal Arts taught animation. The combination of our stop motion project and love for drawing led us to Cal Arts and we became animators.

TODD: That's another trend I see, is that there are some who are crystal clear on what they want to do as an artist, but for most of us it's a process of discovery and a few "a-ha" moments?

TOM: That's very true. When I was a Cal Arts, there were some guys there who were kind of on a second career. They were in their late 20's but realized they wanted to work in animation, so they went back to school to pursue their dreams.

TODD: What are you most excited about right now in the animation industry?

TOM: I hate to say it, but not much. There's a lot of money talk, and business, and layoffs. Not a lot of really fun creative projects. The only shining glimmer just this week is Glen Keane's animated short Duet. It's a beautiful love letter to 2D animation.

Google is highlighting some new technology, but it's really all Glen doing his thing. You can plug tech into it but it's really a low tech thing. I hope the world sees it and says, "Oh my gosh, that's the difference between 2D and CG."

TODD: Another thing I talk about at length in this book is how artists can gain a sense of calling in their work. Do you see your role as an artist as a calling?

TOM: That's a great question. I'll start with a story. I left Disney and went to Big Idea because I wanted to use my talents for God. I just felt that way. Big Idea didn't know how to use me. I had no knowledge of how to use CG.

Then after two and a half years I was laid off. It was a really tough time. My wife and I looked at each other and said, "OK, why did that happen? What was God's purpose here? Did we really leave a mark?" In the middle of all of that, 9/11 happened.

So, all of that combined made me feel worthless. I felt like I had nothing to offer. As a nation we stopped going to the movies and laughing. I felt like police men and firefighters had a calling. They were the ones that mattered. I make cartoons and it does not matter.

It took me a few years to realize that there is value in what I do. People started to laugh again. SNL finally came back on and (then mayor of New

York City) Giuliani came on TV to say it's time to start laughing again and to start healing.

Now our country needed creatives to make us laugh and entertain us. We enjoyed life again. It was a process I went though. There is a calling in what I do. I won't look at my job as more important than a fireman that's for sure. Those guys are heroes. But, I really see the value in what I do now.

TODD: If you had one overarching piece of advice for an artist trying to find their way, what would it be?

TOM: To go out and do it. Don't feel like you have to research, research, research. There comes a point where you just have to do it. As creatives we so often half-bake things because we have so many creative ideas. It's exciting to me that we can develop an idea directly with a small audience. Stop talking and just go out and do it.

TODD: This is really a unique time where you can bypass the gate keepers and build your own platform isn't it?

TOM: That alone; what you just said; is really where I am in my life right now. Trying to find that one thing that I can do as an independent creator. I'm always looking for ways to access my audience more directly.

TODD: Speaking of that, what current project, or venture, are you currently working on and what's the most exciting thing about it?

TOM: Between family, my day job, and freelance, I have very limited time. But I always have projects that I want to move along. I'm still like a creative kid with tons of ideas, but I know I have limited time so I have to focus on a couple of them.

I believe strongly in completing things. Value is when people see it, whether it's good or bad. Then you learn and get better.

I've been putting out a strip every Monday for a year on my web comic OutnumberedComic.com and I still feel like I have my best work in me.

I'm getting older. I'm at the point where I want to do something bigger that touches a lot of people. So, this year I made a goal to start working on a feature film. It's a live action and 2D animation idea that I've been thinking about for a while.

TODD: Every huge project has a Genesis moment and it sounds like you're at that Genesis moment with this feature film project. You mention it all started with setting a goal earlier this year. Are you a big goal setter and if so, how has planning and goal setting helped you in your career?

TOM: I totally do! I believe strongly in making goals. Artists need deadlines and we need goals. Without goals we make great sketchbooks, but we don't make great art. I want to create things that have a release.

I get very nostalgic each year around New Year's (Day). Most of my books were started right at the beginning of the New Year. Around Christmas things slow down and I start planning goals for the coming year. I do it every year.

Some goals don't happen, but overall I hit most of them. This year I'm going to start working on my feature film.

TODD: That's really exciting and I can't wait to see what happens with that. I think you are courageous for putting it out there and declaring it. Any last parting words for an artist trying to find their way?

TOM: Stop talking about it and do it. Move forward. I get dreams, but people need to learn and practice.

I have people saying, "My life long dream is to work at Disney." Then I say, "Well are you drawing every day?" Ninety eight percent of the time they say, "No". In that case it's just a hobby.

If you want to become an Olympic swimmer, don't you think you'd have to get into the pool every day? There are times when I wish I could just be a hobby artist with no deadlines too.

If you say you want to work for Disney, you basically just said, "I want to become a doctor. I want to commit six years of my life in education before I can go and get beat up as an intern."

Many people don't look at it that way. They are wanting to be the best of the best at something. Nobody dreams of being the low man on the totem pole who can't get a job. They dream of being the best. Well, then you have to be the best student now.

Interview with: Amick Byram

Amick sang the role of Moses in the animated feature film, *The Prince of Egypt*. He has sung on hundreds of other films including: *Shrek, Aladdin, Beauty and the Beast, The Lion King, Pocahontas, Hercules, Mulan, El Dorado, The Greatest Game Ever Played* and many others. He is a successful solo recording artist, one of the top session singers in Los Angeles, an actor and a producer.

Amick is a two-time Grammy nominee, soloist for the opening of the Golden Globes, and has had a solo performance nominated for an Emmy. He has voiced over 100 episodes of *The Simpsons*, and is the singing voice of David in *West Bank Story*, which won an Academy Award for best short live action film.

As an actor, Amick starred in many professional stage productions including *Phantom of the Opera*, (Broadway and LA), *Les Miserables*, in the roles of Marius and Enjolras, *Sunset Boulevard* as Joe Gillis playing opposite Glenn Close, and many other musicals and plays from Shakespeare to Neil Simon.

Amick has appeared on prime time television from *Frasier* to *Friends*, and guest starred on *Star Trek TNG* as Ian Troi. Trekkies say his trading cards are worth millions!

Amick has produced theater in NYC at the John Houseman Theater on 42nd St. and is the Founding Producing Director of American Coast Theater Company. He is the President of Oodles World & Entertainment, creating resources and values-based entertainment products for the ever-growing faith & family marketplace.

You can find Amick at:

http://www.amickbyram.com

http://www.imdb.com/name/nm0125974/

TODD: What are some of the most memorable projects you've been a part of, and the most memorable people you've worked with?

AMICK: That is difficult because of the fact that I have been involved in many aspects of the business including theater, music, television and movies. Each has very memorable projects which were fulfilling creatively and also successful. In theater, probably Les Miserables because of the subject matter, the quality and importance of the musical itself on the world stage and my being cast in that musical was a turning point in my personal theater career journey.

In recording, it was the jazz albums in which I received two Grammy nominations but also my own personal music CD project, Encounter, because it expresses the deepest priorities of my heart in a musical style that I feel very comfortable with.

But of all the projects and experiences, I would have to say singing the role of Moses in the animated feature film The Prince of Egypt was extremely significant and memorable. The three-year experience was deep, rich, the people I interacted with were wonderful and dedicated, and the cache' of that project continues to benefit me to this day.

TODD: This may be a tough one to answer, but what do you enjoy more, acting or singing?

AMICK: I actually enjoy singing more because it is more effortless. OK, maybe that tells you I'm lazy! But I actually believe it is my first and strongest gift. I believe I am a good actor and have had critical and commercial success as an actor in both television and theater, but singing has fallen in my lap easier, and seems to be what I am more known for.

TODD: How did you know you wanted to be a vocal artist?

AMICK: I have always sung since I can remember. I came from a very musical family and my brother and sister also sing extremely well. My Mom was the choir director at every church we were ever at growing up so obviously music was a big part of my upbringing.

I didn't actually decide I would be a professional singer until near the end of my third year of college. Up till that point my career aspirations were all over the map...fighter pilot, doctor, etc. It wasn't until I finally realized and admitted that to be in show business as a performer was really the only thing I could see myself actually doing, that I turned the corner and focused exclusively on that one goal.

TODD: As a follow up to that question, what advice would you give to someone who has a wide range of creative talents, in terms of nailing down one discipline to pour their time and energy into?

AMICK: Focus on what you know you are the best at, what you get consistent and sincere support for, what is the most effortless for you and what you enjoy the most at working hard at.

TODD: For someone aspiring to have a career singing, what would you tell them?

AMICK: Decide what area of the music business you see yourself in. What is the film that plays in your head when daydreaming about your life? Is it as a recording artist with a band? Is it in a concert hall with an orchestra? Is it on stage in a musical? Is it in a choir? Is it in an opera? Is it as a session singer only in the studio? Focus your energies and actions on that as an end goal.

TODD: What do you consider to be your life's calling?

AMICK: My life's calling is to use my talents, gifts and skills to have influence in the industry of show business and entertainment so that my life will ultimately be a witness to the attributes of God in that world.

TODD: Has that been a journey of discovery or was it always clear to you?

AMICK: That has always been clear to me since junior high school. My life's calling has always been the same. But how my life's calling is manifested has changed.

Early in my career it was about being excellent enough as a talent to compete and be a professional in the business so that as a Christian I could be salt and light to those around me whoever that may be.

Now, it is about being excellent enough to compete in the creation and production of entertainment products that ultimately point people towards the attributes of God; and that my life will be salt and light to those around me whoever that may be.

TODD: What has been the most difficult thing for you about working in your industry?

AMICK: The unfairness of it all. There are no guarantees and it is unlike any other industry or business where if you do A and B well, you will likely be rewarded with C.

TODD: What has been the most enjoyable thing for you about working in your industry?

AMICK: The incredible, smart, creative and educated people I get to work with all of the time.

TODD: What is one overarching piece of advice you would give to any young creative trying to find their way and discover their calling?

AMICK: For everyone, after you have determined you want to test your talents in the marketplace, you must have a tremendous amount of passion and drive to be in the business. You must also have an outstanding work ethic.

As a Christian, make sure this is God's calling for your life. Don't presume that because you get lots of compliments when you perform that this is what God wants you to do for a career.

TODD: Lastly, what's it been like to have a spouse (and children) with similar talents? Share with us a little about that if you would.

AMICK: For me, it has been and continues to be a great journey with my wife Cassie. We have managed to have a fairly normal life. Of course in show business I don't think any of it is really all that "normal" in the whole scheme of things.

However, we have a great relationship, have a happy home and have raised two boys to successful adulthood. They are both in the music business and we are able to continue to pour into their lives.

God has richly blessed our lives, our marriage, our careers, and we are both better because we have each other for support, we use each other as sounding boards and as a stabilizing force. With both of us being in the business we understand intimately the struggles we individually go through. God continues to watch over us and protect us. With God, all things are possible.

Interview with: Cassie Byram

Cassie Byram began her professional career in entertainment at the age of 19. An award winning actress, singer, songwriter, Cassie's career encompasses theater, film, television, voice-overs, published song writing and multiple album releases for adults and children alike. Her many stage roles include Marguerite in *The Scarlet Pimpernel*, Christine in *Phantom of the Opera*, the Narrator in *Joseph and the Amazing Technicolor Dreamcoat*, Mary in The *Glory of Christmas*, and Maria in *West Side Story* for which she received a Backstage West Critics Award for Best Actress.

For two years, Cassie guest-starred on the T.V. series, *Jake and the Fat Man*. She co-starred in the pilot episodes of *Star Trek: Deep Space Nine, Journey to the Center of the Earth* and *Civil Wars*. You can also see her in the feature film, *The Time Changers* with Gavin MacLeod and

Jennifer O'Neil. Cassie is featured singing the solo "If I Loved You" in the film City Hall starring Al Pacino, and was honored to work with the highly respected film director, Hayao Miyazaki as the featured soloist for the classic animated film, *Totoro*.

Cassie is the creator of the Lifetime Scripture Songs, which she co-wrote with her son, Jonathan Byram. Her new, upbeat album release "Wonderfully Made", and the original lullabies of "Sweet Dreams" feature key Bible verses set to original music for kids that parents will love too!

Cassie is now the Executive Creative Producer for the family entertainment company, Oodles World. She describes her greatest accomplishments as being a wife and proud mother of her two boys.

You can find Cassie here:

http://cassiebyram.com

http://www.imdb.com/name/nm0125977/

TODD: What are some of the most memorable projects you've been a part of, and the most memorable people you've worked with?

CASSIE: Most Memorable Project - Playing Maria in West Side Story early on in my career was the most fulfilling project I have ever been a part of. The beauty of the music by Stephen Sondheim and the depth of the role of Maria is what every actress lives for. That alone would have been enough, but I was also blessed to receive a critic's award that year for Best Actress. The other three actors I stood on the platform with at that ceremony were Jon Voight, Julie Harris, and the late Jack Lemmon! I couldn't believe it!

Most Memorable Person - I have truly been blessed to work with so many memorable people in this business so it's hard to choose, but I would have to say one of the most remarkable was Julie Andrews. I was absolutely awestruck when I met her, and the idea that I would be working with her was somewhat nerve wracking. After all, she really is the kind of iconic super star in this business who will go down in history. She was of course the ultimate professional, but she never ceased to impress me with her kindness and humility. Although I was the understudy, I had the awesome privilege to sing a duet with her. It is a moment I will never forget.

TODD: This may be a tough one to answer, but what do you enjoy more, acting or singing?

CASSIE: I have a deep love and passion for music, so this is a tough choice but I would have to say what I actually enjoy doing most is acting.

They both require hard work, study, practice, and especially discipline, and both are incredibly rewarding when performing, but the reason for my choice is because of the limitless possibilities I feel I have as an actress to create an experience for the audience with the spoken word, or even when not speaking! Acting is also how I first discovered my love of performing.

TODD: How did you know you wanted to be on stage as an artist?

CASSIE: When I was 11 years old my 6th grade teacher saw something in me. At mid-year she gave me the lead role in an original show. It was a take on the Cinderella story. I played Cinderella as an Indian princess whose face was scarred as a little girl. She was treated unkindly until one day a prince falls in love with her, scars and all.

I'll never forget how it felt to convey a message of hope and illuminate the human condition in that way. I also felt a natural confidence in what I was doing. Add applause to that and I was hooked!

TODD: As a follow up to that question, what advice would you give to someone who has a wide range of creative talents, in terms of nailing down one discipline to pour their time and energy into?

CASSIE: Many of us in this business have a range of creative talents, that's the blessing and the curse. The trick is to discover what you're most natural gift is and develop that to it's utmost. Pay attention to what keeps working for you and what you get the most approval for. Once you figure that out, stick to it.

TODD: For someone aspiring to have a career singing, what would you tell them?

CASSIE: Don't take whatever talent you have been given for granted. Many people feel that they were born with a good voice and they don't need to do anything else to develop it, but know this; there are other people out there with comparable gifts going for the same exact jobs that you are.

Make sure you hone your skills with classes and instruction from experts in your field. Know your craft and practice it. The saying "use it or loose it" is very true. You don't want to find yourself presented with an opportunity, only to blow it because you were rusty and unprepared.

I would also highly recommend acquiring a deep knowledge for yourself of your particular discipline. Understand methods and techniques. Know who came before you. Whether it's singing or any other talent, be as familiar as you can with as many projects and artists in your field as you can. Show respect for what you do and you will be given respect in return.

TODD: What do you consider to be your life's calling?

CASSIE: I do believe I was called to be a performer in the entertainment industry, but more importantly, I am called to allow God to work through me in my chosen profession, no matter what that happened to be.

Because I am living proof of the transforming power of the Love of God, my true passion is to convey that in everything I do, whether it's with my marriage, the way I raise my children, the kind of daughter I am, the kind of friend I am, or the way I conduct my career. That is my life's calling.

TODD: Has that been a journey of discovery or was it always clear to you?

CASSIE: LOL. Definitely a journey of discovery!

TODD: How have different seasons of life impacted your creative journey?

CASSIE: Once I had children they became my first priority. Having children is with out a doubt one of the greatest blessings on this earth, but it also changes everything.

If you are pursuing a career in show business, especially as a performer, be sure you enter in to that part of your life "eyes wide open".

Otherwise, you will suffer, your marriage will suffer, and worst of all, your children will suffer too. Understand the sacrifice that it takes and be sure you are willing to make it!

Having said that let me also say that if it is God's timing it will be the most fulfilling thing (along with your marriage) that you will ever do.

TODD: What has been the most difficult thing for you about working in your industry?

CASSIE: Rejection. Everyone tells you not to take it personally, but it's just so hard not to…at least for me!

TODD: What has been the most enjoyable thing for you about working in your industry?

CASSIE: I really enjoy giving people a moving experience. Causing people to reflect on life and to feel something is a thrill. That's why live theater is such a joy. I get to experience those moments right along with the audience. It's like conducting the emotions of thousands of people at once with just your music and story. Having the joy and privilege of doing what I love for so long is a blessing I will always be grateful for.

TODD: What current project, venture, or event are you currently working on and what's the most exciting thing about it?

CASSIE: My most current project and also the one I am proudest of is a collection of songs I have co-written with my son Jonathan called Lifetime Scripture Songs.

We have released two albums so far, our lullaby album called SWEET DREAMS, and our up-tunes album entitled WONDERFULLY MADE. We are planning to complete the set with a third one.

These are songs for kids and their families with bible verses as the lyrics. I am so happy with the music and very excited about the benefit of scripture memorization for young children. This is music that parents enjoy too, so the whole family can learn these songs together just by making it the sound track of their lives while the kids are young.

I'm humbled and happy to say these songs are available in many Christian bookstores, on iTunes, at Oodlesworld.com and on my website at cassiebyram. com.

TODD: Is there anything else you would like to say to artists, or anything else you would like to mention or talk about?

CASSIE: There is so much I would like to say to anyone thinking about pursuing a career as an artist, but I'll just put it this way... be ready and willing! Be ready to join a community of deeply passionate, talented, volatile, exciting people. Be ready to get beat up and disappointed on a regular basis. Be willing to fight to maintain who you are, but also, be willing to grow. In the end, if this is what you are called to do, it will all be worth it.

TODD: What is one overarching piece of advice you would give to any young creative trying to find their way and discover their calling?

CASSIE: Always bring you're "A" game. Be the absolute best you can be in all that you do. It's hard work, but again, it's worth it.

I love this quote from Bishop Charles Blake, Senior Pastor of West Los Angeles Church of God in Christ.

"Capacity and ability constitute accountability and responsibility. We should never be pleased to dwell on a level of existence lower than that on which God has made it possible for us to dwell. We should strive to be the best we can be and to reach the highest levels we can reach. To do less is to be unfaithful stewards of the life entrusted to us." I can't say it any better than that!

TODD: Lastly, what's it been like to have a spouse (and children) with similar talents? Share with us a little about that if you would.

CASSIE: I wouldn't have it any other way. I am so proud of my husband and very supportive of his talents and pursuits as he is of mine. We've had the joy of each other's success and helped each other through the tough times. We have also been very fortunate to work together on a regular basis.

It's never easy of course. A marriage between two artists is fraught with unique challenges. It takes real dedication and devotion to the commitment of marriage in order to survive. I can honestly say that my husband and I are partners in this life.

The fact that both of our boys are professionals in the music business absolutely thrills us. We have the greatest discussions when we get together about all of our latest experiences. It's really fun for us as a family that we have this common interest and passion. There is no doubt that this is God's calling on all of our lives.

Interview with: Kathleen Cooke

Kathleen Cooke is a media professional, an award winning actress, and along with her husband, Phil, is a founding partner at Cooke Pictures, (cookepictures.com), where she is a key creative leader and oversees casting for all major projects. Together, in 2013, they launched The Influence Lab (influencelab.com) focusing on redefining the Christian mission strategy in the digital age.

She is the editor of the monthly Influence Women Newsletter, influencelab.com/women, and her weekly blog can be found at kathleencooke.com which focuses on developing, connecting and inspiring Christian women involved in media, entertainment and other areas of influence.

She co-directed the Biola Media Conf. from 2007 to 2011 at CBS Studios growing it to be one of the largest conferences for Christians working in secular entertainment and media in the US.

She founded and directed Christian Women In Media/West Coast/ Hollywood from 2011 to 2013, and is presently an adjunct professor supervising student interns in Hollywood for Asbury University.

She is on the advisory board for the Hollywood Prayer Network, and Hollywood Connect, and speaks, teaches and consults on various topics centered around faith, media and influence both nationally and internationally.

You can find Kathleen here:

http://kathleencooke.com

http://www.cookepictures.com

TODD: Kathleen, like many creatives' you have a breadth of creative talents which have led you to work in different roles during different seasons. You've worked as an actress, and a writer, but you are also the Co-Founder and VP of Cooke Pictures, you're a speaker, and you have experience in production management, casting, and so many other areas of entertainment and media production. Tell us a little about your creative journey and how you got to where you are today.

KATHLEEN: I grew up in Las Vegas, Nevada in the 60's and 70's and the classical arts were nonexistent. My favorite toy growing up was an outdoor trash can full of secondhand clothes that I used for costumes. I made up my own stories and performed for hours in the backyard of my house. Theatrical acting was just in my DNA.

I was also a people pleaser and my journey took me into other professional avenues for a time. With the encouragement of my husband and our move to LA in 1991, my passion for acting took a big jump. I dove into the professional business as a working actress in Hollywood for many years doing commercials, plays, and small films. I now oversee casting and am a member of the creative team at Cooke Pictures in Burbank, CA.

TODD: You seem to have always had a heart for the student. Your work with the Biola Media conference for many years, and your experience helping students and graduates from various creative arts schools, says a lot about your passion to mentor and equip others. How and when did this become a passion of yours?

KATHLEEN: Yes, besides directing the Biola Media Conference for 5 years, I was an adjunct professor in the Cinema and Media Arts department, and I am currently an adjunct for Asbury University directing and assisting media interns on studio lots and production offices throughout Hollywood.

Teaching for me has also been a huge part of my life journey. I even taught 7 years of elementary school after graduating college. I continue to speak and teach to young professionals both here in the US and in many foreign countries each year. I believe it is our responsibility to see the next generation thrive and become successful. I love working with students and seeing them find new avenues and ways of sharing truth, light, and beauty on big and small screens.

TODD: What do you enjoy most about working at Cooke Pictures?

KATHLEEN: I am thrilled to see that the projects we produce change lives, make a difference in our culture, and bring insight and truth to viewers. I also love the mix of projects our company creates from theatrical films, documentaries, commercials, and digital media to website development, branding, and consulting.

TODD: You are also still very involved in conferences and events as a speaker and a planner. What do you enjoy most about that?

KATHLEEN: I love seeing the creativity of people when the light goes on. I am honored to be given the privilege of sharing some insights, guidance, and direction from things I have learned along my life's journey. It's so cool to see and hear how something I shared started a creative engine, sparked a change, and resulted in a new direction in someone's life

TODD: What do you consider to be your life's calling?

KATHLEEN: To follow the lead of Jesus and GO into ALL the world and bring His truth and light using the gifts and talents He has given to me. And then, to encourage others to do the same.

TODD: Has that been a journey of discovery or was it always clear to you?

KATHLEEN: It's always been a constant and continual journey and I am always discovering new things. My husband is an explorer and that's why I fell in love with him. But I am his biggest cheerleader. I pray our love for exploration never dies until we take our last breath.

TODD: How have different seasons of life (marriage, motherhood, career changes, etc.) impacted your creative journey?

KATHLEEN: My life seasons have all impacted my creative journey. As an artist every experience you have changes your perspective and gives you new insights.

I have always told young actors to be a better actor, experience as much as you can. Go to museums, theatrical plays, events and shows. Take time to travel, talk to people who are different from you, experience different cultures, and eat weird things.

They all add to a richer and broader perspective in your work and life. Certainly, what I knew in my 20's about life, love, marriage, kids and career is vastly different from what I know today. The way I approach and the focus of my work, craft, and art has all been impacted by my life seasons. The secret is to embrace each season and enjoy the ride because life changes quickly.

TODD: What is the toughest thing about the entertainment industry right now?

KATHLEEN: Our young college grads think they can make a film, write a million dollar script, or be the next big star just because they went to college for 4 years. LA is flooded with naïve, self centered, entitled "wannabees." They don't think they have to put the time and hard work into really learning the craft, laying down a good foundation, and building a career. They want it instantaneously. We live in a culture that is enthralled with technology and lacking in the ability to know how to tell stories, and actually create. They just re-create.

TODD: If you had one overarching piece of advice for artist/creative trying to find their way, what would it be?

KATHLEEN: Over deliver. Hollywood is a narcissistic community for the most part. It's an "all about me" culture. Build relationships by being humble, willing, and then once you get the job over deliver.

If they ask you for one script give them 3. If they want you to show up next week with your lines memorized show up this week with them memorized. The over prepared, dedicated, and willing souls will always rise to the top. Those are the ones that do it because they love it and not for how much they are getting paid. Those are the ones driven to excellence.

TODD: What current project, or venture, are you currently working on and what's the most exciting thing about it?

KATHLEEN: I have been spending the last few years traveling around the US and world (12 countries in the last 2 years) speaking and teaching media professionals and students on various aspects of the media industry. My husband, Phil Cooke, and I launched our new nonprofit "The Influence Lab" (influencelab.com) and I am overseeing Influence Women. My passion is to gather women and unite our talents and gifts to work together around the globe to see change happen.

I co-direct the new yearly ASCEND Women's Conference (ascendconference. org in LA), edit the monthly Influence Women newsletter, and write a weekly blog all designed to unite women and inspire, encourage, and educate them on how they can make an impact, create change, and make a difference within their own fields of expertise.

TODD: Is there anything else you would like to say to artists, or anything else you would like to mention or talk about?

KATHLEEN: Stay alert, don't get lazy, and rock on! The best is yet to come. Oh… and have fun and laugh a lot!

TODD: Life for the creative is a journey and we respond to opportunities as they arise. That being said, do you set career or development goals? If so, how has planning and goal setting helped you in your career?

KATHLEEN: I believe it is important to have a plan, make specific choices, and then regularly re-evaluate yourself as to whether or not you are progressing.

It's easy to get stuck in a job that pays well and keeps your bills paid, but doesn't get you where you want to be in the long term.

I have also found that the best goals have led me to further growth and come with risk. Keeping yourself financially unencumbered is one of the best goals you can do for yourself and usually the hardest to achieve in our culture of never having enough.

But, if you can resist the need for "stuff", it will allow you to take more risks and give you more options toward reaching those hard to achieve goals.

For me, long term goal setting is about keeping regular reachable goals, and keeping them flexible, growing, and forgiving. Strive for the best, shoot for the stars, face into the wind with a specific course heading, but don't let your goals rule your life either.

Learn to enjoy the richness of the entire journey. Remember, some of those set backs to achieving your goals may actually be God's leading to a better path and direction that you can't immediately see. He sees the future and holds the keys to eternal joy and true success. His leading, and you following it, should be your ultimate goal.

Interview with: Phil Cooke

An internationally known writer and speaker, Phil Cooke has actually produced media programming in nearly 50 countries around the world. In the process, has been shot at, survived two military coups, fallen out of a helicopter, and in Africa, been threatened with prison. And during that time – through his company Cooke Pictures in Burbank, California – he's helped some of the largest nonprofit organizations and leaders in the world use the media to tell their story in a changing, disrupted culture.

According to former CNN journalist Paula Zahn, Phil is rare – a working producer in Hollywood with a Ph.D. in Theology. He's appeared on NBC, MSNBC, CNBC, CNN, Fox News, and his work has been profiled in the New York Times, The Los Angeles Times, and The Wall Street Journal.

His book *"*<u>Jolt!: Get the Jump on a World That's Constantly Changing</u>*."* shares his secrets of making today's culture of disruption and change work for you. "<u>One Big Thing: Discovering What You Were Born to Do</u>" helps you find the great purpose and calling for your life – and was named by the Washington Post as one of the Top Five Business Books for 2012. His new book is "<u>Unique: Telling Your Story in the Age of Brands and Social Media.</u>"

He has lectured at universities like Yale, University of California at Berkeley, UCLA, and is an adjunct professor at the King's University in Los Angeles. In addition to writing his blog at philcooke.com, he also blogs for The Huffington Post, and is a contributor to Fast Company, Forbes.com, and FoxNews.com.

You can find him at:

<u>http://philcooke.com</u>

<u>https://twitter.com/philcooke</u>

TODD: Phil, you're a media producer, brand guru, author, thought leader, speaker, and more. Which of those roles have you enjoyed the most and why?

PHIL: I love writing. In fact, my greatest regret is that I didn't start writing sooner. I'm a preacher's kid from the South, and no one in my family took writing seriously. My dad was a scholar - he had about 6,000 volumes in his library - but didn't own a single novel. As much as he loved to read, he didn't encourage me to write.

It wasn't until I was thrown into writing for television advertising in my thirties that I realized I had some talent. Honestly, I think it cost me a significant part of my career. My dream since college was to direct feature films. However, had I realized that my real gift was writing, I would have focused more (and earlier) on writing and producing.

TODD: I read your book "One Big Thing: Discovering What You Were Born to Do", I really enjoyed it and have recommended it to my readers as well. What comes to mind as a key principle from that book that can specifically help artists discover or clarify their calling?

PHIL: Stop pursuing your passion. I meet people on a weekly basis who are passionately pursuing a career for which they don't have a shred of talent. Just the other day a writer sent me a film script. She told me how passionate she was about writing for the movies, and as I read the script I realized it was truly awful.

I say let's focus less on passion, and more on discovering where your talent really lies. Once you realize what you "wired" to do, and what you're terrific at, then the passion will come.

TODD: Some creatives are laser focused in a niche market or at least gravitate to one clear discipline,...but many artists I talk with, have several creative abilities and have a hard time choosing one. What advice would you give multi-talented creatives having a hard time identifying one discipline to pursue?...or do you think that's necessary?

PHIL: The idea behind my book "One Big Thing" isn't that your one big thing isn't necessarily a "job." It's more of a calling, a purpose - the overarching reason you're on the earth. When you figure that out, you'll find many ways to express it. I feel that my one big thing is helping Christians engage today's culture more effectively. To accomplish that we've launched a nonprofit called "The Influence Lab" (influence lab.com), I speak on the subject, write, and more. Your "one big thing" isn't about just being a secretary, a coach, or insurance agent. It's much bigger than that, and how you express it is up to you.

TODD: OK, this question is for my video producer friends. Once an artist finds their industry, there are still hundreds of choices within that industry. How did you make the decision to be a video producer for non-profit organizations?...vs. going after something else like directing feature films or something of that nature?

PHIL: Directing feature films was my original goal, but my first opportunity to produce and direct was in the non-profit world. I realized I had a gift for that, and doors kept opening. By my thirties I had filmed in about 30 countries around the world – and in some very risky situations.

Did I get sidetracked from my original goal? Possibly. The bad news is that I'm not doing what I dreamed of early on. The good news is that in nearly 4 decades of doing it, I've never once missed a paycheck, won a cabinet full of awards, and helped our clients do some awesome things in the media.

TODD: As a follow up to that question, how did you initially become interested in video production and how did you initially break into the industry?

PHIL: I made Super-8 movies in high school with some friends. We produced war movies, mafia movies, space movies - all kinds of very elaborate stories. When I went to college I took my camera thinking I might find others who would want to do the same thing. (I had no idea it was something I'd eventually do for a living.

In fact, I enrolled in college as a music major.) When I was unpacking on my first day at school, a couple of those films fell out of my suitcase and a friend across the hall said, "Hey - I'm taking a film class and I can show you how to edit your movies." (I was so ignorant I had no idea you could actually cut the film).

So that night we were working late in the university film department, and the professor happened to be there. After watching a few minutes over my shoulder he asked if he could show my little movie to his film class. I said yes, as long as I could sit in the back of the classroom.

The next day he showed the film to the class, and although it was pretty awful, they had a long discussion about it. Then - quite unexpectedly - the thought hit me like a bolt of lightening - that if I could do something with a camera that made people talk like that — then that's what I'm supposed to do with my life. It's the most crystal clear revelation I've ever had in my life.

I changed my major that afternoon, and have never looked back.

TODD: I like for readers to see that well known creatives are human too. What has been the most difficult thing for you about *working in your industry?*

PHIL: Aside from the usual stress about your next project, or worrying how you'll pay the bills, I think the biggest frustration is educating nonprofit and ministry leaders about media. When I work in secular advertising or in Hollywood, studio executives and ad agencies get it. They know what you're talking about and want to make things happen. But sadly, seminaries don't train pastors and ministry leaders in the media. So one of the most challenging parts of my job is the initial client education into why the media matters, how much influence it has in the culture, and why Christians should embrace it.

TODD: Which of your books is your personal favorite and why?

PHIL: I don't really have a "favorite" but:

"<u>The Last TV Evangelist</u>*" is the most fun.*

"<u>Unique: Telling Your Story in the Age of Brands and Social Media</u>*" is what I'll be remembered for (if I'm remembered at all.)*

"<u>One Big Thing: Discovering What You Were Born to Do</u>*" is the reason I get so many emotional thank you notes from people who feel like they're finally discovered their purpose and how much it's changed their lives.*

TODD: What are some of the most memorable projects you've been a part of, and the most memorable people you've worked with?

PHIL: I've been involved in PBS event specials, ESPN extravaganzas, Super Bowl commercials and more. But "Starting Over" was a Billy Graham television special that I'll never forget.

The ministry came to us and said they wanted to do something completely different, and we accepted that challenge. In fact, the show opened with a guy in his car committing suicide. It was evident early on that this would not be a typical Billy Graham show, and during editing, the ministry leadership from that time came to our editing room three times very upset.

They hated it. When we finished, they put it on the shelf and said it would never be broadcast. But by the grace of God a ministry leader's wife happened to pick up the screener, pop it in a machine and look at the show. We learned that an hour later, with tears in her eyes she told her husband, "People need to see this."

So they broadcast the program on schedule worldwide, but buried it as the middle night of a 3 night broadcast, hoping few would see it. But the Los Angeles Times reported that 2.5 billion people worldwide saw the program, and it generated 1 million calls for salvation. I've been told was the most successful religious or inspirational program in history. Stories like that keep you going.

TODD: One thing I have always liked about you is that there doesn't seem to be a separation of sacred and secular. You don't hide your faith, but you don't impose it on people either. It's a very genuine approach to living as an artist and thought leader. What advice would you give to artists about how to approach their particular world view in their art?

PHIL: Lead with your talent, not your testimony. When people are impressed with your ability, they'll listen to anything you have to say. But if you try to share your faith without first winning their trust, they'll never listen.

TODD: IF you had one overarching piece of advice for an artist trying to find their way, what would it be?

PHIL: Do it everyday. I met a girl in college who's goal was to be a concert pianist. She practiced four hours a day. The question becomes, how many hours a day do you practice your craft?

I meet people who call themselves "writers" who rarely actually write. Directors who rarely direct. Guess what? You're competing with people who take art seriously. If you're not serious, go sell insurance. It will be a lot easier.

TODD: What current project, venture, or event are you currently working on and what's the most exciting thing about it?

PHIL: The Influence Lab – no question. Certainly we're developing some new television projects at our production company Cooke Pictures in Burbank, but the purpose of the Influence Lab is to teach and train the next generation of Christians in the media.

We've done that in India, Russia, Spain, The Middle East, South America, South Africa, and many other places. It's incredibly exciting for me to see this many Christians around the world, so excited about sharing their faith through the media.

Right now we're at the funding stage because I can't afford to continue paying for it out of my pocket. But there's no question that this will be an important focus for the rest of my life.

TODD: If you had to say one last thing about creativity, what would it be?

PHIL: Someone once said that the key to having good ideas, is having a lot of ideas. Too many people write one screenplay and expect that to be their ticket to the big time. Others produce or direct a couple short films and think that will propel them to feature films.

Ask any respected writer, and they'll tell you they have a drawer full of screenplays, short stories, and ideas that they'll never show anyone. A creative artist needs to work through the kinks and develop their talent. The more ideas you generate, the better chances of one catching fire.

Interview with: Shea Fontana

Shea Fontana is a freelance writer and programming consultant. She has worked for The Walt Disney Company, Kabillion, PorchLight Entertainment and more. Her credits include work on shows like "Doc McStuffins", "The Secret Saturdays", and "Sushi Pack".

You can find Shea here:

http://www.imdb.com/name/nm2865415/

http://www.sheafontana.com

https://www.linkedin.com/in/sheafontana

TODD: Shea, you've had experience as a staff writer for Disney and other companies, as well as some fantastic freelance gigs. Which do you prefer and why?

SHEA: While being on staff certainly has it's perks (free coffee and Reese's Pieces! Steady paycheck! Insurance!), I enjoy the freedom and diversity of freelance. I'm the type of person who likes to get up early and immediately start writing when my mind is fresh and most offices would frown upon me staggering in at dawn in my pajamas.

With freelance, I'm usually working on several projects at once so I never have a chance to be bored. If I get stuck on one project, I can work on another while my subconscious works out the issues. Plus, if I want to go for a run at 3:00, I can and don't have to ask for anyone's permission.

TODD: How did you first become interested in writing and what made you choose children's programming as your market?

SHEA: I always wanted to be a writer. When I was a kid, I would come home from school and spend all afternoon writing stories imitating Laura Ingalls Wilder and other books that I read.

In college, I started out thinking I'd go into journalism, but then I'd spend my evenings watching SpongeBob, Home Movies and Foster's Home for Imaginary Friends. I realized that animation was the place for me. I have a silly sense of humor and enjoy writing things that are fun and hopeful.

TODD: In your opinion what are the 2 or 3 most important things a script writer should understand?

SHEA: In animation, writing has to be very visual and precise. If the storyboard artist can't understand exactly what the writer is seeing in his or her head, then the jokes will be muddied and the story unclear. Far more so than in live action, each image has to written on the page.

Also, every writer needs to understand that everyone's first draft is terrible. It's so easy for writers to get down on themselves, but even the most successful writers do a lot of rewriting between the first draft and the final product.

I recently read an early draft of an animated movie that made a ton of money and was critically acclaimed. When comparing this early draft to the actual movie, I realized that most of the plot and nearly every line had changed. I find it comforting that even writers who are immensely respected turn in drafts that aren't perfect and have to be rewritten.

TODD: What has been the most difficult thing for you about working in your industry?

SHEA: In a lot of ways, the US animation has shrunk. With vertical integration at the networks and international production companies offering budgets that US studios just can't compete with, there is only a handful of domestic buyers for any project. But on the flip side, we've only seen the tip of the iceberg in potential for animation series online. As online video viewing develops, more opportunities will arise for animated content.

TODD: What are some of the most memorable projects you've been a part of, and the most memorable people you've worked with?

SHEA: Every project has taught me something and expanded my skills. I love the joke-driven, wacky comedy of "The 7D" which was an experience that taught me to write fast and consistently.

Doc McStuffins is a wonderful project because I know that every script I've written will really affect someone. The issues and emotions explored in Doc McStuffins have the ability to shift kids' thinking and help them feel less alone and more understood.

TODD: You also have a great understanding of how the kids TV industry works in terms of US and overseas distribution, funding, and that sort of thing. What advice would you give to writers and other creatives about learning the business side of creativity?

SHEA: Animation is a global industry and it's a medium that travels well throughout the world. It's incredible that you can go to Nairobi or Beijing and kids know SpongeBob.

Since independent producers often have to cobble together financing for a series by getting several international broadcasters aboard, they must develop shows that will work for a worldwide audience.

Even the networks take a global view to programming. Disney operates over 100 channels across the world, so they are looking to get the most bang for their buck by creating shows that they can air worldwide.

I would encourage creatives to become familiar with the worldwide market and not just the US market. There are so many opportunities globally that can be overlooked.

Personally, I've written for a French production company and developed a show with a Chinese company. Surprisingly, many international shows are written in English, then translated for other markets. Many writers make a living exclusively off of international productions.

TODD: In addition to writing scripts, you also have development experience. What do you enjoy more, helping develop a concept or writing episodes for an existing series?

SHEA: Development is a lot of fun because you can take a big picture view of a series. In development, you get to plant the seeds of the characters and stories that are fully realized during the writing process.

Development and writing are incredibly intertwined and overlap in a lot of ways. I love the episodic writing experience because I've had the opportunity to work with lots of amazing people.

In episodic writing, you get emulate the creative voices of incredibly talented people while bringing your own brand of crazy and fun to the project.

TODD: If you had one overarching piece of advice for a writer or creative trying to find their way, what would it be?

SHEA: My advice to writers would be to read scripts and watch cartoons. There's no substitute for learning the jargon, rhythm and story structure of an animated show.

I love reading scripts. You can find lots of scripts online and if you're in LA, you can go to the WGA library to read scripts. Just yesterday, I went to the WGA library to read some Frasier scripts. The more you read, the more tools you'll have in your writing arsenal.

TODD: What current project, venture, or event are you currently working on and what's the most exciting thing about it?

SHEA: I have been working on a few live-action family movies. It's a different space for me and it's been fun to explore the opportunities and limitations of live action as compared to animation.

TODD: Is there anything else you would like to say to artists, or anything else you would like to mention or talk about?

SHEA: I think one of the best things that writers and artists can do is be open to new experiences and take in everything you can. You can't create without those seedlings inside of you. Read books, watch TV, go to improv shows.

What might be seen as "leisure" to an accountant is the life breath of the creative. I can trace the premise for an episode I wrote of The 7D called "Jollywood Jam" to the night my husband and I went to the opera. You never know what might get the wheels turning so experience as much as possible.

TODD: Life for the creative is a journey and we respond to opportunities as they arise. That being said, do you set career or development goals? If so, how has planning and goal setting helped you in your career?

SHEA: I'm definitely a goal oriented person. I try to work on my own projects alongside my paid work and I always have a weekly goal for pages written. I don't always meet my goals, but it does keep me focused and heading in the right direction.

I think freelancers have to be especially good with goal setting because there's no higher up to keep you motivated. You're the only one looking out for you so it's imperative to keep focused on your goals.

Interview with: Heather Martinez

Heather's credits include work at Nickelodeon Animation Studio (Storyboard Artist, Writer), Walt Disney Television Animation (Director/Show Runner) Nickelodeon Creative Resources (Illustrator) Simon and Schuster (Illustrator) Random House (Illustrator) and more.

Heather started her career working at Nickelodeon on *SpongeBob SquarePants* and eventually found herself as the Director of Disney's, *The Replacements*. Upon starting a family, Heather decided to work as a freelancer and worked as a storyboard artist for Nickelodeon on *Fairly Oddparents* and *Tuff Puppy* as well as several well known projects as a book illustrator.

You can find Heather here:

http://www.imdb.com/name/nm1610443/

http://heathermartinez.blogspot.com

TODD: Heather, you have a wide range of experience from visual development and art direction, to storyboarding on shows like The Fairly Odd Parents, Kick Buttowski, and of course Sponge Bob. You also have experience as a director on The Replacements. Which of those roles have you enjoyed the most and why?

HEATHER: I think I've enjoyed being a writer slash storyboard artist the most. Most of the shows I've worked on you're not only developing the show visually shot-by-shot as a story artist, but you're also putting words into the characters mouths.

You work from a general outline of the show and work from that. Creatively speaking that puts a lot into the hands of the artist. We worked like that on My Life As A Teenage Robot, and of course SpongeBob. Dialogue driven jokes sometimes fall flat with kids but they love visual comedy, so writing and boarding like this is really effective.

TODD: What first got you interested in the animation industry?

HEATHER: My younger brother Carl used to draw and I used to watch him. Eventually Carl became a magician, but I stayed with drawing. I went to a magnet school called The Orange County High School of the Arts and we were doing animation in the 9th grade.

TODD: Wow. Super jealous. What was that like?

HEATHER: It was great. We had annual film festivals and the competition even at that age was really intense.

TODD: How many of those students moved on to Cal Arts or started working in the industry?

HEATHER: I graduated high school in '95 on the heals of Lion King, and at that time the studios were really on a hiring binge and some of the really talented kids were hired right out of high school. I wasn't quite ready for that.

TODD: At what point did it hit you that you could work in animation for a living?

HEATHER: I always got in trouble in elementary school for drawing too much, but when I went to Roland I thought I had to be an animator and I didn't really like animating.

There was a guy from Dreamworks that came in and was asking me what I wanted to do. I told him I didn't really want to be an animator. He said, "You don't have to be an animator. What do you want to do?" I said, "I guess I'd want to be a storyboard artist." He said, "Then be a storyboard artist!" I didn't think that was a career but he told me that you could actually train to be a board artist.

TODD: I love hearing stories like that where, even if for one meeting, where an experienced artist intersected the life of a young creative and gave them some direction that suddenly opened up new possibilities for them. Was that this moment for you?

HEATHER: It was. It made a big difference because I liked telling stories visually, but I never quite connected with animation.

TODD: You've worked in studio and as a freelancer. Which do you enjoy more?

HEATHER: That's tough. Both are so different and have different rewards. I miss the day-to-day interactions the studio provides and I miss learning from colleagues, but I would not trade being home with my kids or the flexible schedule for anything. My new colleagues now throw cheerios on the floor and run around singing "Let It Go". (Pause) Actually, now that I think about it, my animation colleagues aren't that different from my kids.

TODD: In your opinion, what are the main tools a freelancer needs to succeed?

HEATHER: Freelancing assumes you know what you are doing from the get-go and your kind of flying solo. For example, I was doing this project for Disney Consumer Products and I did a bunch of work that was set up wrong. They walked me through the correct way to set it up and were very gracious. But that's not the norm.

You usually can't "learn on the job" as a freelancer. You also really need connections. You really need to be reliable. You want to be that person that turns it in on time and in good quality.

TODD: What was most challenging or surprising about the transition from visual development and art direction to working as a director?

HEATHER: It was a bit of a shell shock. I went straight from board artist to show runner. It was downright scary. It was also a different studio. From Nick to the Disney lot. The iconic building with the dwarves you know.

Suddenly I had to know how to direct people on a very tight budget. It was magic, but hard. I went from MLAATR which was very board driven as I mentioned, to the Replacements which was more of a sitcom format. I started on the pilot, then it got picked up.

TODD: I have a chapter in this book about seasons and how artists need to understand them. You've had some interesting seasons working your way up the industry, but you also did something courageous, and you decided to stay at home to raise your kids.

The crazy thing is you did this at what some would say the pinnacle of your animation career. You were directing for the Replacements when you made this decision. Can you tell us a little about that?

HEATHER: I think it was Paul that said "I know what it is to be in need, and I know what it means to have plenty, and I have learned the secret of being content". I think I learned that to an extent working my way up in animation. Then after 10 years of marriage we finally got pregnant.

After my daughter was born I signed her up for the day care on the Disney lot, but then one day on my maternity leave I really wondered if I would miss seeing her season 1 or season 2.

Animation would always be there but my little girls seasons 1 and 2 would only happen once. A really dear friend of mine, who was a homeschool mom, actually came to me at that time and said, "In your life you'll have opportunities to create many masterpieces, but your children are your magnum opus."

So, it was actually a really easy decision for me at that point and we're now in season 6 of the Savannah show, and we have little spin-off called Jacob who's coming up on a year now.

TODD: How has your creative background come in handy in raising a family?

HEATHER: I homeschool so it helps with creativity and crafts, but I also do character voices when I read and Savannah loves it.

TODD: Another thing I talk about at length in this book is how artists can gain a sense of calling in their work. Do you see your role as an artist as a calling?

HEATHER: I see it as a blessing. I see homeschooling as a calling. I wrestle with that question because animation is so much fun, so I definitely see it as a blessing.

TODD: What are the top two or three key things a director has to know?

HEATHER: When I first stated directing, I felt like Kung-fu Panda in the scene where he first meets The Furious Five and is just in awe. I was working with and hiring people that worked on The Smufs, and Nightmare Before Christmas, and Iron Giant, and others that worked on so many shows.

But I felt like Po because I had to become the Dragon Warrior overnight. I had to set aside hero worship and try to lead. Directors need to know how to manage people. You need to keep your team and the executives happy. You have to work with people and make a show happen.

Many artists don't get that kind of training involving human interface. You also need to learn how to communicate your creative ideas and critiques in a way that is productive and understandable.

TODD: If you had one overarching piece of advice for a creative trying to find their way, what would it be?

HEATHER: I would say, be humble, be good at what you do. Those things are all valid but the older I get I want to say to young people, "Let the Lord to be your director." In entertainment it's so easy to lose your way. When you get into the day-to-day grind, it's easy to become a people-pleaser.

Not everyone follows the Lord, but if you do, make sure he's the director. I know you love your job. I know you love the people you'll work with, but love God more. If you are a Christian, love your colleagues enough to tell them about Christ.

TODD: Do you set career or development goals? If so, how has planning and goal setting helped you in your career?

HEATHER: If you want to get anywhere, you need a map. The GPS may change your route, but the end point is always there. Having a goal is that end point.

At the same time, my walk as a Christian is different and you really need to keep submitting that goal to the Lord. He'll take you thru some twists and turns but in the end you'll be more amazed at what He can do.

TODD: What current project, venture, or event are you currently working on and what's the most exciting thing about it?

HEATHER: I've been working on developing an illustration style for some children's books I'm working on. I'm collaborating with a friend's daughter to write some character-focused stories in sort of a Dick and Jane style.

TODD: Is there anything else you'd like to mention or talk about?

HEATHER: Stay the course. Animation is a great career and calling but there are days when it will just feel like a job and it's temporary. Live for eternity.

Interview with: Michael Maurer

Michael is a professional Film & TV writer/story editor/developer specializing in kids and family entertainment for both animation and live action.

In FILM: Michael has been commissioned to write or has optioned 10 feature films (including one produced.) His most recent projects include a 3D animated feature for Starz Animation (based on his original idea), and a TV animated feature for Toonz Animation, based on the classic *Speed Racer* franchise, which is currently in production.

In TV: Michael has written over 300 animation and live-action scripts, story edited series and developed series bibles for companies such as Disney, Universal, Warner Brothers, and a dozen international companies. His most recent projects include scripts for A Squared Entertainment's new Warren Buffett series, *Secret Millionaires Club*, airing on HUB, and *Pac-Man: The Adventure Begins*, now airing on Disney XD.

You can find Michael here:

http://michaelmaurer.wordpress.com/

http://www.imdb.com/name/nm0561041/

TODD: You've had an extensive career as a writer and have worked on a wide range of iconic shows. You've also written some features. Which (TV or feature films) do you enjoy more and why?

MICHAEL: Personally, I prefer feature films. I like to tell one big story, take the hero on a journey and have him change in the end. But most of my work is in TV animation, which is also great.

TODD: In your opinion what are the 2 or 3 most important things a script writer should understand?

MICHAEL: First and foremost, story structure. There are certain axioms that hold true to most stories and it's vital to know them as a means of developing and editing your work. There are a lot of good teachers out there, David Freeman, John Truby, etc. Also vital is character development.

You have to know who your hero is, his goal, his flaws, what is driving him in the story. Lastly, theme is vital. What moral argument are you as a writer trying to present to the audience through your story?

TODD: What has been the most difficult thing for you about working in your industry?

MICHAEL: Freelancing. Always pounding the pavement, dealing with overlapping deadlines. It's not like it was when I started out. Back then there were a lot of staff jobs.

TODD: What are some of the most memorable projects you've been a part of, and the most memorable people you've worked with?

MICHAEL: What comes to mind is Gummi Bears, Disney's first TV animated series. It was so exciting to be on a show with great animation and top notch voice actors.

Disney's Darkwing Duck was a blast to work on, but my favorite was a CBS/ Nelvana series called "Mythic Warriors," a 26 episode, fantasy adventure anthology based on the Greek Myths.

TODD: What advice would you give to writers and other creatives about learning the freelance and business side of creativity?

MICHAEL: *If you're not already in the biz, you need to write great sample scripts that stand out above the others. Once you've got a few calling cards, find a producer or story editor or agent who is willing to read a script. If you're stuff is good, it will rise to the top.*

If you're already a professional, keep pounding the pavement, make new connections, promote yourself, go to industry events, anything to expand your reach. As far as the business side goes, it's a necessary evil. It's a different hat so you either have to be versed in it or have an agent.

TODD: In addition to writing scripts, you also have development experience. What do you enjoy more, helping develop a concept or writing episodes for an existing series?

MICHAEL: *Tough question, my viewpoint changes all the time. Truthfully, the key factor is how much I like the project. I get some really badly developed ideas on my plate and it can be difficult to turn them into saleable ideas.*

It's a challenge which is fun, but I far prefer working with producers who know what they are doing and have great concepts. It's always a fun change of pace to write scripts, and writing consistently for a show is more stable and preferable.

TODD: If you had one overarching piece of advice for a writer or creative trying to find their way, what would it be?

MICHAEL: *Study story structure. Analyze great films or series as to how they applied what you've learned. Write!*

TODD: What current project, venture, or event are you currently working on and what's the most exciting thing about it?

MICHAEL: Can't talk much about the current projects, but I recently wrote two TV animated features for Toonz, a studio in India. I had the freedom to develop my own stories based on their characters. Great fun and successful result.

TODD: Life for the creative is a journey and we respond to opportunities as they arise. That being said, do you set career or development goals? If so, how has planning and goal setting helped you in your career?

MICHAEL: Yes, I do set goals, which are primarily based on my screenwriting aspirations. The challenge is to keep the work-for-hire jobs from preventing me from doing spec projects. It's always important to set goals, and to put them there again if they at first fail to materialize.

TODD: Do you see your career as a calling? Why/Why not and how has that impacted your career decisions?

MICHAEL: I do believe that writing is a calling for me, that there are moral issues that need to be expressed thematically via film and TV. The challenge is finding time to do my own spec projects where I can control the value of my work.

TODD: Is there anything else you would like to say to artists, or anything else you would like to mention or talk about?

MICHAEL: Purpose, Passion, Practice, Persistence. Those are the "four Ps" to success in this biz.

Interview with: Ashley Postlewaite

Ashley is the Co-founder/Executive Producer for Renegade Animation. She has produced hundreds of commercials and over 100 half hours of episodic television (including episodes of *The Mr. Men Show, Hi Hi Puffy Ami Yumi,* and *The Tom and Jerry Show*) as well as a few movies.

You can find Ashley here:

http://www.renegadeanimation.com

http://www.imdb.com/name/nm1041234/

TODD: What made you decide to start an animation studio (along with Darrell Van Citters)?

ASHLEY: Darrell and I were at Warner Bros and both of us had always imagined having our own companies someday, so having worked together there, we decided that we'd strike out on our own together.

TODD: How did you first become interested in animation?

ASHLEY: My background was live theatre, which I fell in love with at the age of 7. By the time I graduated from college I had done hundreds of plays, and loved the producing side of things, so I thought that TV and film might be the logical next step – and might actually allow me to pay my rent and eat.

I happened to get a freelance job producing a symphony concert called Bugs Bunny in Concert for Warner Bros…and through that met Darrell and began learning about animation. I immediately fell in love with the art form, and the artists. They felt very much like theatre people to me – dedicated to their craft, passionate about it, a little bit wacky, etc.

TODD: So it sounds like you had some childhood interests that gave clues to what you would do someday?

ASHLEY: Yes, my major interest growing up was the theatre. I absolutely loved doing plays. Everything about it. Working in box office, hanging the lights, sewing *the costumes, you name it.*

Every summer I spent all day every day at the theatre, and couldn't have been happier. It was the perfect training ground for me.

TODD: What's the toughest thing about your job?

ASHLEY: Hmmm, I guess the hardest thing about my job is the rare occasion when someone isn't working out and I have to let them go. I hate it, but I know it is an important part of keeping the company strong.

TODD: What's the most enjoyable thing about your job? The people!

ASHLEY: What's the most memorable project you've worked on? That's really hard to say. After 22 years of Renegade, the memorable projects just keep on coming. I'm proud of our work on all of them.

TODD: What trends do you see that artists should be aware of as they prepare for a career?

ASHLEY: Being computer savvy at the same time that you are trained well in traditional fundamentals is the winning combination. You really need both skill sets to be employable in the industry today.

TODD: Life for the creative is a journey and we respond to opportunities as they arise. That being said, do you set career or development goals? If so, how has planning and goal setting helped you in your career?

ASHLEY: I do set goals, but as you say, this kind of career also pivots on opportunities as they arise. Early on in the company I had specific financial goals and when we met them I rewarded myself by purchasing a piece of artwork, as I had a long term goal of having an art collection.

That has worked well. Setting a goal is always a good thing, as it gives you something to focus on and can serve as a motivating factor. Holding oneself accountable for working toward the goals is the key.

TODD: What advice would you give to someone who has a wide range of creative talents, in terms of nailing down one discipline to pour their time and energy into?

ASHLEY: I'm not sure that one discipline is the way careers are going to work anymore…but if it seems that focusing on one discipline is necessary, I would think about the one that you lose yourself in when you do it.

When does time stop and the world become quiet? That's the discipline for you. It is such a joy to watch artists work at the thing that they love to do – and that love always shows in the work they produce.

TODD: What does a typical day look like for an executive producer?

ASHLEY: There are no typical days! But, in general, my days are filled with a lot of interaction with our production teams – meetings to check progress against production schedules, trouble shooting specific production issues as necessary, meetings with clients, etc.

Then there is the solitary stuff like budgeting new projects, handling corporate business items, etc. My Dad asked me once what I actually "did" in my job. After thinking awhile I said, "I don't know Dad, I just talk on the phone a lot." In some ways, what I really meant, was that the real job day-to-day of an executive producer (at least in my case) is THINKING.

I make decisions and try to be as smart as I can possibly be given whatever challenge, project, or mountain is in front of me, and in so doing, give our crew the leadership they deserve. AND I have always thought that the most important thing a producer can do is to create a nurturing and happy environment for her artists.

TODD: What are the main things you look for when hiring someone?

ASHLEY: Darrell is always looking for the artistic quality of their work. Then, if that passes his standards, we're looking for the person to be pleasant, calm, collaborative, dedicated, and respectful of others. If you have those qualities, you'll be a good Renegade.

TODD: For someone just beginning their career who has aspirations to start their own creative business someday, what advice would you give them now?

ASHLEY: Study business, read books by successful entrepreneurs, continue to hone your craft, and save your money during the good times so you can weather the bad times.

Also – find people who are successful and talk to them…ask them questions, shadow them for a day (with their permission!) Go to work in the kind of business you might like to start – and try to learn every single aspect of that business. Start at the bottom if you have to – but just get yourself into the environment and soak it all up.

TODD: Leading and running a studio can be wonderful, but it can also be tough at times. What are some of the risks, and some of the rewards?

ASHLEY: The risks, I suppose, are the obvious ones – that you'll fail and lose a lot of money, that it will be harder than you thought it would be, and/or, perhaps that you won't be able to cope with the uncertainty, pressure, or stress that comes with owning a business.

But I would argue that all of those things (except, perhaps, losing lots of your own money) can also be risks of working for someone else. People get laid off every day.

As for the rewards – they are many! You have some degree of flexibility that you wouldn't have working for others, you have the freedom to create the culture that you want your company to have, you can decide who you want to have working for your company, and at the end of the day you can feel very proud of having founded and run your own company.

TODD: What current project, or venture, are you currently working on and what's the most exciting thing about it?

ASHLEY: We're doing a lot of work for an educational client right now and there are a number of exciting things about it. We feel great to be doing work that will help young children learn and grow.

From a production management side it is a huge number of small pieces moving through our system, which has required some creative thinking in terms of tracking and managing that work. It's fun to be challenged in that way.

We're waiting on a season two pick up of the Tom & Jerry show, which we are producing for Warner Bros (airing on Cartoon Network) and we are very excited about that.

We've also had a series of commercials for Der Wienerschnitzel which have been an absolute blast to work on. They are very retro and cool – right up our alley.

We've got a couple of pilots in the works, too – which is always exciting and fun as you get to really make an impact on how a show takes shape, and there is the underlying possibility that it will go to series!

TODD: Is there anything else you would like to say to artists?

ASHLEY: Just that if you want to be in this business, then GO FOR IT! You will be surrounded by talented, funny, fantastic people every day. I know I am.

Interview with: Stephen Silver

Stephen Silver was born in London in 1972. Aspiring to be a professional artist his whole life and knowing drawing would be his vocation, Silver got his professional start in 1992 drawing caricatures in amusement parks.

Since then, he has worked as Character Designer and Supervisor for Disney Television Animation, Sony Feature Animation and Nickelodeon Animation, designing characters for *Kim Possible, Danny Phantom* and Kevin Smith's *Clerks* the animated series, to name a few.

Silver has a live brick and mortar school in Los Angeles called Silver Drawing Academy, and also teaches an online correspondence course where he provides his students with a better understanding of the Character Design process and provides the tools needed for a career in the art business through Schoolism.com. Silver names three treasures to success in life that give him what it takes to keep on drawing: determination, passion and desire.

You can find him here:

http://www.silverdrawingacademy.com

http://stephensilver.blogspot.com

https://twitter.com/stephensilver7

TODD: Stephen, you're an amazing character designer, industry thought leader, author, artistic app developer, and now art teacher through Silver Drawing Academy. Which of those roles have you enjoyed most and why?

STEPHEN: I really have enjoyed all of them, because they have all offered a learning experience, It is all part of the creation process. I find what I truly enjoy the most is teaching, Simply because it just feels good.

TODD: Years ago I picked up your book, "The Art of Silver, Vol. 1" and one thing I really love is that you put some of your early drawings in there so people could see that skill level progresses with practice.

I talk to so many artists who see other artists work and they feel defeated. What advice would you give an artist who has an interest or passion, but doesn't yet have the skill level they desire?

STEPHEN: They are not alone, we see the finished product of any professional success and think it is automatic and it just happened, it never does. It's a journey that you embark on, make some mistakes along the way.

Know that if you are willing to work on your craft, you will improve as long as you are open minded and learning about what you are doing wrong so you can correct yourself as you continue to practice.

TODD: In your opinion what are the 2 or 3 most important character design principles?

STEPHEN: Shape variation, Construction, and Feeling.

TODD: What has been the most difficult thing for you about working in your industry?

STEPHEN: *The most difficult thing I would say is not knowing what the next gig is. It is a nomadic life, pooping from one place to the next. you must be prepared for this.*

TODD: What are some of the most memorable projects you've been a part of, and the most memorable people you've worked with?

STEPHEN: *I really enjoyed Kim Possible and Danny Phantom, They were just great experiences, I learned a lot about my art during those years, Trying to figure out new ways of drawing and designing, it is always a bonus if the shows become a hit, Your work becomes memories of somebodies' childhood which is pretty cool.*

In the industry you make lots of friends. I was always fond of three of my directors, Bob Doucette, the director that first hired me into this industry and believed in me. Chris Bailey on Clerks the animated series and Kim possible, he really pushed Butch Hartman and I on Danny Phantom. He was inspiring.

TODD: In your bio, you mention three treasures that keep you drawing: determination, passion and desire. Can you briefly elaborate on those a bit?

STEPHEN: *This is not a career where you can be lazy. It requires determination to push you through your goals you must set, it requires passion, because you have to love what you are doing or you will give up to soon. It requires the desire to dream big and see yourself enjoying and having fun in this artistic life.*

TODD: What first drew you to character design (as opposed to background design or some other discipline)?

STEPHEN: *I loved drawing people and caricaturing. It is really all character design is. So it was a perfect fit. I had no idea what a character designer was when I was hired as one. But it made sense that this would be the best position for me.*

TODD: What current project, venture, or event are you currently working on and what's the most exciting thing about it?

STEPHEN: *I just recently opened up my very own school in Los Angeles where I teach Character Design and Caricature figure drawing, this has been really exciting. I have been working independently for years now and I freelance on various projects.*

If they seem fun, I'll do it. If not, I won't. I focus a lot on my family and spend lots of time with them and am just taking it easy. My mission is to "Spend a calm life."

TODD: How can independent artists and studio owners like us use our influence to help creatives thrive?

STEPHEN: *Simply by spreading the messages through book form or videos and hoping that others who believe in it will share it too. Don't be afraid to be open and discuss what you believe is right.*

Interview with: Narina Sokolova

Narina has had a long and extensive career in the animation industry. With a background in fine arts and painting her skills have led her to work for Nickelodeon, Cartoon Network, Warner Bros. Animation, and Disney on such shows as *Johnny Bravo, Rugrats, Kid Notorious, The Buzz on Maggie, My Gym Partner's a Monkey, Out of Jimmy's Head,* and more recently *The Looney Tunes Show,* and the incredibly popular and critically acclaimed *Micky Mouse Shorts.*

You can find Narina here:

http://www.narinasokolova.com

http://www.imdb.com/name/nm2600818/

TODD: What first got you interested in the animation industry?

NARINA: I was always fascinated by animation as an art form. It's like creating a whole World. Everything is in animation. And working in this industry full time seemed like the best career choice I could make.

Also, animation seems so have ever-expanding possibilities. It has a great future in my opinion.

TODD: Looking back, what childhood clues do you see that were indicators of what type of career you might go after?

NARINA: Visual arts was easiest path for me. Ever since I was young, it was very apparent to everyone in my family that i could draw well. I seemed to create images effortlessly. I did try to study violin, but it was too difficult. :)

TODD: You've worked in studios and as a freelancer. Which do you enjoy more?

NARINA: It's hard to say because there have been so many interesting projects. Sometimes you do art work for even a small project that turns out to be very special.

TODD: In your opinion, what are the main tools a freelancer needs to succeed?

NARINA: To have an open mind and try to turn even a small project into a great opportunity to learn and advance. Think of it as a personal work of art. Work at it and enjoy it.

TODD: What brought you to the US from Russia? What was that transition like?

NARINA: It was challenging but very exciting and liberating to be able to learn so much, to have all this freedom, and to have so many opportunities. I feel very fortunate in so many ways to have come to the US when I was so young.

TODD: What are some of the most memorable projects you've been a part of?

NARINA: Almost all the of the projects I was part of are memorable in their own way. It's an experience of creating something new. Even when there are stylistic or schedule limitations it can be fun to accept the challenge and invent a new solution each time.

TODD: Do you feel that you were born to be an artist? Why or why not?

NARINA: I feel very fortunate to be able to work and make a living in the creative arts industry.

TODD: How did you know you wanted to work as a background artist as opposed to a character designer or some other animation art career?

NARINA: I have a fine arts and design education. I was a traditional painter before I got into the animation industry. It seemed like the most natural choice for me.

TODD: What would you say are the key things an animation background artist should know?

NARINA: Design skills are most important. Drawing and painting skills as well. It's also very important to use software in a creative way.

TODD: If you had one piece of advice for a fine artist or background painter trying to start a career, what would it be?

NARINA: Try to always have fun and enjoy creating art.

TODD: What show or project are you working on right now?

NARINA: Mickey Mouse shorts at Disney. Fantastic project!

TODD: I love the new Mickey Shorts. The art direction, timing, comedy, and connection to the Disney roots are fantastic? What's been the best part about working on those shorts?

NARINA: An incredibly talented crew and supportive management! I also love the freedom to experiment with new styles. It's always challenging and never gets boring. I've been working on them for two years but it feels like only a couple of months.

TODD: What does a typical day look like for a background designer?

NARINA: You choose an assignment, meet with an art director to discuss ideas about it, then you just get to play with shapes, textures, and colors all day. :)

TODD: What is your typical process for designing and painting a background?

NARINA: It varies depending on the project. Rough design usually starts after the composition and staging are established in the animatic.

Next, you design and stylize the scene, decide on the painting style, lighting, and overall visual language. You also have to figure out the best way to use software to achieve what you have planned.

TODD: Do you set career or development goals? If so, how has planning and goal setting helped you in your career?

NARINA: I set some basic overall career goals then respond to opportunities as they come. I just want to keep working. The industry and the world are changing so fast, you never know what will inspire you next.

TODD: Do you still work in fine arts? Do you put your work in any galleries?

NARINA: I do still paint and draw when I have time or feel inspired and I occasionally have gallery shows.

Interview with: Marcelo Vignali

Marcelo Vignali is one of the most respected production designers, art directors, and visual development artists currently working in the world of animation. Formally trained as an illustrator, Marcelo has helped create many classics throughout his 25-year career, such as Disney's *Mulan, Lilo & Stitch, Brother Bear*, and Sony Pictures Animation's *Surf's Up, Cloudy with a Chance of Meatballs*, and *Hotel Transylvania*.

Marcelo has twice been nominated by the International Animated Film Association for Production Designer of the Year, once for his work on *Surf's Up*, and again for his work on *Hotel Transylvania*.

Marcelo is currently working at Sony Pictures Animation, and lives in Southern California with his wife and two daughters.

You can find Marcelo here:

http://vignalistudio.blogspot.com

http://www.imdb.com/name/nm1825684/

https://www.linkedin.com/pub/marcelo-vignali

TODD: Marcelo, you've had an amazing career. Your training as an illustrator has served you well and it seems you've had a natural progression in that career as you have moved into visual development, art direction, and now production design for several feature films.

Was that your plan or did you just keep working at your craft and looking for opportunities?

MARCELO: No, although it seems like that in hindsight, my career has certainly gone in a different direction from what I expected way back when I was going to art school.

When I went to art school it was sort of like the dark ages for animation. You have to think about the context of the time, by 1983 several animation studios had already gone or were going under.

Filmation was just about to go out of business, Hanna-Barbera really wasn't doing much. I think they were doing Scooby Doo and Scrappy Doo, and Disney was in the process of being bought out and junked (fortunately that didn't happen).

So the idea of having a career in animation really wasn't feasible, and I had a lot of art instructors telling me that animation was something I shouldn't go into.

So, I decided I would major in illustration. But, fortunately I was very stubborn and I decided that my illustration style was to create illustrations that looked like they came straight out of an animated film.

You see, working in animation was something that I've always wanted to do, and I was going to do it regardless whether there was an industry or not. I was NOT going to take "no" for an answer!

When I got out of school in 1987 I started shopping my portfolio around to different illustration houses and a friend told me about DIC Entertainment, a new animation studio in town. They were doing all preproduction here in the US, but farming the work out to Asia in order to get their production animation work done.

I took my portfolio there and was hired. Ironically enough, a year later in 1988 Who Framed Roger Rabbit came out, and then shortly after that (in 1989) The Little Mermaid hit the theaters.

There was a huge resurgence of animation, and I was at the right time at the right place. I had a portfolio that already looked like it was geared for animation.

I think this is a testament to believing in yourself and sticking to what it is that you believe. I was going to work in the field of animation whether there was an animation industry or not.

Fortunately for me the animation industry took off right around that same time that I was starting out in the business, so it was very fortuitous for me.

TODD: How did you first become interested in drawing and what made you choose animated features as your career goal?

MARCELO: I can pretty much pinpoint my interest in animation to that moment my mother took my brother and I to see Disney's Fantasia. That movie did so many things to me, it made me laugh, it terrified me, and most of all it inspired me. After that, I was hooked on animation.

TODD: In talking with you, one of the things that has really impressed me is that you are an artist to the core.

You frequent museums. You draw constantly. You can talk about creative topics for hours. You're always trying new mediums. You even host a weekly sketch club with other artists. This is really a lifestyle for you isn't it?

MARCELO: Yes, art is not what I do, it's who I am. There is no separation between myself as an artist and myself as a person. They are one and the same. We all have talents, and it's important to discover what those talents are and utilize them to the fullest.

TODD: How important is that for artists?

MARCELO: Gosh, it's the core. Artists aren't like doctors or lawyers. (No disrespect to those professions.) But, a true artist is always working. We are constantly analyzing the world around us, and recording it.

I even took my sketchbook on my honeymoon — I can't imagine a doctor studying surgical techniques while on holiday. People giggle when I say I took my sketchbook on my honeymoon, but it seemed as natural to me as packing my toothbrush.

TODD: Another thing that I noticed is that you are unselfish with your knowledge and experience. You willingly speak at conferences, mentor younger artists, and rub shoulders with people from all walks of life. What drives you to do that sort of thing?

MARCELO: *Well, that certainly is a personal mission of mine. When I was younger I couldn't find a mentor that could take me under their wing and help to guide my career. So, whenever a professional would open up to me, I cherished their words and advice.*

Now, I'm in a position where I can be a mentor to someone, so I try to be the mentor I wanted to meet when I was younger.

Also, I want to pass the knowledge I've learned along to the next generation so that it doesn't disappear. What we do as artists is bigger than any one person, in the end all we really do is contribute to that creative process for a short time -- and then we leave this world.

What could be better than inspiring other artists to become a part of that wonderful process that has meant so much to me?

Also, I think it's my Christian duty. Matthew 7:7 "Ask and it will be given to you; seek and you will find; knock and the door will be opened to you."

TODD: Why do you think creativity is so powerful and so important for people and culture?

MARCELO: *I believe art is the reflection of our humanity. We see our own humanity (or inhumanity) contained within the artwork we create. That's why I take it so serious, and why I believe artists have a responsibility with their art.*

TODD: In your opinion what are the 2 or 3 most important things a concept artist must know?

MARCELO: *First, a concept artist is a professional. Never forget you're being paid for your professionalism. Never miss a deadline.*

Second, always do your best. That's what it means to be a professional. Never miss a deadline.

Third, always keep your promises. Never miss a deadline.

TODD: What are some of the most memorable projects you've been a part of, and the most memorable people you've worked with?

MARCELO: The most memorable projects for me are really about the people I've had a chance to work with. Working on Mulan was a dream come true for me, in part because of all the wonderful talent on that film. But, that's the thing about each film I've worked on. They each come with their own unique experiences and challenges.

TODD: What has been the most difficult thing for you about working in your industry?

MARCELO: I would have to say having to navigate office politics. The best advice for anyone starting out in the business is to simply ignore office politics and concentrate on the work. Let others deal with the politics; you just concentrate on having fun.

TODD: What has been the best thing about working in your industry?

MARCELO: I think the best thing has been the many friendships and relationships I've built. The people I've met have been a tremendous blessing to me.

TODD: If you had one overarching piece of advice for a writer or creative trying to find their way, what would it be?

The best advice I can give anyone considering animation as a profession is to have-fun! The word Animation means the state of being full of life or vigor; liveliness. What could be more fulfilling and joy-filled than being part of a process that creates animation? So have fun!

CHAPTER 13

Planning Informational Interviews and Tours

Freedom lies in being bold.

Robert Frost

In developing your plan, once you pick an industry and list a few potential careers from that industry, I recommend you do some informational interviews and (if possible) some on-site company or studio tours. I'll walk you through how to connect with key people, studios, or companies to request interviews and tours. Below are the steps and some scripted lines that you can use as a guide (or exactly as they are written).

- **Step 1:** Make a list of five companies, studios, or organizations in your area of interest that you would benefit from were you able to visit them.

- **Step 2:** Research them online and connect with key contacts thru social media (LinkedIn, Twitter, etc.).

- **Step 3:** Contact them to see if they offer tours to groups or individuals.

I have found it most effective to connect thru social media then request a tour or informational interview because you can craft your message well. The more professional and honest you are, the more likely you are to land a tour or informational interview.

Requesting a Tour

If however you have to call the company, here is a script you can use.

Hello. My name is (your name here) and I am a(n) (senior in animation school, freelance illustrator, graphic designer, etc.) and I'm trying to learn all I can about this industry. I'm going to be in your area soon and I was wondering if you allow (students, artists, etc.) to briefly tour your facility. (Pause for answer. Also, take note of their name if they provide it at anytime.)

If they say yes.

That is fantastic. Thank you so much for your help (their name). Is there a certain number I should call or person I should email to figure out the best day and time, or is that something you can help me with?

If they say no.

No problem. Thank you so much for your help (their name). I did have another question. Is there someone there, preferably in my specific area of training, who may be available sometime for a 10 minute informational interview?

If you hit a brick wall, keep trying other ways (without being annoying) or move on to your next studio of choice.

Informational Interview

Before I started Timbuktoons, I landed a few informational interviews with various animation leaders (studio heads, producers, etc.) To be honest, I was surprised at how willing they were to share. I was turned down a few times, but was able to land enough informational interviews to gather some great information before starting my own venture.

Here are some tips and general questions (which you will need to customize and add to depending on your specific industry and situation). Once you define your target industry and career track, I recommend doing a web search for "informational interview for (enter your career track here)" and you'll be able to find some great questions for your specific area of interest.

Tips

- Be extremely professional and courteous. Remember they are willingly giving you some of their time.

- Let them know you will only take 10 or 15 minutes of their time and be sure to stick to that time frame unless they specifically say they would like to keep going.

- Be positive and upbeat.

- Keep questions generic in areas that may be a bit too personal (such as salary, or questions about failure/mistakes)

- Spend a short amount of time on small talk, then get into the interview. This shows you value their time.

- Don't do any overt marketing. This isn't a sales call.

- Follow up with a "thank you" email, or better yet, mail a hand written card.

General Questions

- What experience did you have prior to your current position?

- What kind of education did you have?

- How many hours do you work in a typical week?

- What is the culture like there?

- What's the toughest thing about your job?

- What's the best thing about your job?

- What type of personality is needed for a position like yours?

- Looking back, what are some things you would do differently?

- What are the busiest times each year?

- What is the salary range for your profession?

- What advice would you give to someone with my experience level?

Even today, after 25+ years in the creative industry, I still attempt to tour animation studios, creative agencies, and creative conferences whenever I find myself in a new city on business or pleasure. Being a professional artist is a constant journey of learning and expanding your knowledge and experience pool. That's what's so exciting about the creative life. Once you know what flavor of creative you are, there's something else to consider.

CHAPTER 14

Seasons

Everything has seasons, and we have to be able to recognize when something's time has passed and be able to move into the next season. Everything that is alive requires pruning as well, which is a great metaphor for endings.

Henry Cloud

Aside from pin pointing which "S" of the the S5 Audience you find yourself in, it's also vital for your planning and goals to determine and understand what season of life you find yourself in.

This question relates to things such as age, financial status, marital status, whether or not you have children, and other factors. The key thing here is to embrace your season for what it is. It's easier in some seasons to take risks, move to a new city, or go back to school.

While your season may seem inhibiting, you have to embrace it for what it is, and trust that all of the things that may seem like barriers are simply guides to your growth during this season. I have found that life's timetable is often different than what we prefer.

I've also found that just about everything that ever crossed my creative horizon has come into play at a later season than I expected. In short, any identity and calling cues that you have sensed will likely come into play at some point. Random things that don't make sense early in your career, will likely eventually line up and make sense.

One other thing I should mention about seasons. I've noticed that most artists' careers are broken up into 2 overarching mega-seasons (with many mini seasons in each).

1. **PYD Season: Paying Your Dues**

2. **RTR Season: Reaping the Rewards**

Don't get me wrong. Both seasons take hard work. Both seasons have challenges and curve balls. However, there is a distinct difference between the two. There's no exact time frame for the duration of each season. For many, the transition is identified by a major career move.

The PYD Season is characterized by rapid change, searching for your artistic voice and niche, gaining experience, developing key relationships, learning as you go, and discovering what you love and what you hate.

The RTR Season is characterized by working smarter not (quite) harder, great self awareness, working from your core strengths, maximizing time, wanting to make things count, wanting to do something big, wanting to work in things that have the most traction, being a thought leader, mentoring others, and wanting to give back. For many this occurs near the middle age years.

I mention those two key overarching seasons just to put them on the radar of young artists as they begin to plan and strategize. You can't plan the details of your life for both seasons, but knowing that these mega-seasons exist will help artists be aware of where they are currently and what's coming next.

Lean into your season and learn from it. Set yearly goals that push you closer to your long term career goals and never give up. Perseverance and dedication to your craft are key. This brings me to the next point.

CHAPTER 15

Freelance, Studio, or Go Into Business?

If you come to a fork in the road, take it.

Yogi Berra

Which you choose depends on calling, season, location, and industry. I recommend working at a studio or some type of creative environment at least for a few years before you attempt to venture out on your own as a freelancer or business owner. You'll gain valuable experience and further clarify what you want to do long term.

It's wise to freelance while you are looking for a full time creative position, but I usually don't recommend freelancing as a career choice right out of college. You still need some on the job training and experience that will serve you later on down the road. Freelancing requires that you already know what you are doing and assumes that you have reached a level of proficiency that enables you to offer a service with a strong level of confidence.

In the animation industry it's common for studios to crew up for a production or series, then lay off artists when production goes into hiatus. It can be a tough way to live, but the positive is that you can gain a lot of experience from different studios in a few short years.

The time to take risks which you can more easily bounce back from is definitely before you get married and start a family. It's much tougher (though not impossible) to take big risks or go back to school once you have these responsibilities.

Risks are still necessary and healthy even when you have a family. However, you must carefully weigh the options, count the cost, and discuss it with your loved ones as you consider various decisions that will impact them. If you are person of faith, prayer is essential.

The choice between freelance, working for a studio, and going into business for your self also depends heavily on your personality, experience, industry, and career goals. Below are some key considerations for the 3 options.

Considerations for a Freelancer

- How does my identity and calling inform me in the pursuit of this avenue in my creative career?

- Do you have enough experience, connections, industry in-roads, case studies (portfolio), to be a successful freelancer?

- Do you understand the tax implications, business practices, pricing benchmarks, and barriers to entry?

- Have you spent some time building up clients on the side (while still working a full time salaried job) to make the leap to a freelancer?

- What does your personality and history reveal about how successful your big decisions are?

- What do those close to you think about it?

- Have you counted up the cost? What financial or relational obligations do you have that could be at risk from this career move?

- Have you talked to at least 3 other freelancers in your specific field or career track?

- Do you have the proficiency, perseverance, work ethic, communication skills, and people skills to be successful?

- Where do you live? How does this impact your plans?

- What target markets can you successfully go after?

- Am I prepared to run a small business? (Freelancers are essentially 1 person businesses.)

(Also see next chapter: Tips for Freelancers)

Considerations for Working In a Studio

- What does my identity and calling tell me about pursuing this avenue in my creative career?

- What experience will I gain by working at this studio? (early in your career, experience is more important than salary.)

- Is this a company I want to work for short term or long term?

- How does working for this studio fit into my overall career goals?

- Does this studio have a successful track record?

- Does this studio have a healthy culture?

- Will I be able to support myself and my obligations by working at this studio?

Considerations for Starting Your Own Creative Business

- What does my identity and calling tell me about pursuing this avenue in my creative career?

- Have I always had an entrepreneurial spirit (even small scale)?

- Am I a risk taker by nature?

- Do I understand what it takes to run a small business?

- Have I talked to at least 3 other creative business owners?

- Do I handle change well? (Not the jingly kind.)

- Do I have a business plan?

- Do I have enough working capital?

- Have I spent adequate time working in this industry?

- Do I have the experience, clients, connections, and contracts needed to make this a success? (According to analytic and data research site, Bloomberg, 8 out of 10 businesses fail within 18 months.)

Hopefully, those questions along with the identity, core values, and calling work you have worked thru while reading previous chapters, will help spark a thought process that helps clarify which avenue to take at this season in your creative career.

CHAPTER 16

Tips for Freelancers

The dictionary is the only place where success comes before work.
Vince Lombardi

Chances are that as an artist, you will find yourself working as a freelancer at some point in your career (either in addition to a salaried job, or instead of one). Therefore, this chapter is well worth reading for every artist.

Some projects require on-site freelancers, some remote. Some projects are long term like working on a 13 episode animation series. Some projects are short term or one-off projects. It also depends on your location.

As I mentioned above, LA, NY, and Atlanta (to name a few) have studios that crew up for production, then go on hiatus for a few months until the next season moves into production. Location is a catch-22. There are more opportunities for freelancers in these cities, but there is also more competition. Some freelancers use agents while others do not.

Because of technology and the internet, I think right now is the best time ever to be a freelancer. Last summer, for example, we crewed up to 17 people for 4 months, but only 4 of us were onsite. The rest of the artists were all over the country, and even included freelancers from

Brazil and France. We often use voice artists who have online demo reels and high quality recording capabilities at their homes.

Our interactive and game development partners are 2000 miles away from us on the west coast, and most of their programmers are in Europe (which is nice when you want to send off animation at the end of the day, then wake up the next morning and see that it is already programmed and integrated into an app or game beta).

Here are 7 tips for breaking into your industry as a freelancer.

1. Secure basic financial stability and live modestly.

Creativity and financial pressure do not mix. You may have to work a part time or full time job doing something other than your dream job while you build clients and learn your trade. Working somewhere in a creative field close to what you want to do is preferable but not always possible as you start out.

2. Clarify your calling and key marketable skills.

Make sure you are working in your sweet spot. Your sweet spot is where your passion, calling, skills, and marketability intersect. Consider targeting a niche market. I have a good friend who works primarily as an illustrator for the toy industry. He does other work, but he intentionally targets that industry and it has served him very well.

3. Set long term career goals. (Also see Section 5)

You can't develop and work a plan, or even take steps in an intentional direction unless you have an idea of where you are trying to go. Years ago when I worked in print design we would always start with the print date, then work backwards to set milestones to build a schedule. Think of your career like that. Where do you dream of being someday? What needs to happen for you to get there?

It may not happen just how you plan, but at least it gives you a plan of action. President Dwight D. Eisenhower once remarked, "Planning is useless, but the process itself is indispensable." What he was saying is that, plans usually don't work out how we envisioned, but the plans were essential for providing forward movement, along with a sense of direction and purpose. Planning helps you clarify your calling.

One caution here. When it comes to taking action toward your career goals, don't get to overwhelmed with all that has to happen, just focus on the main goal and identify the next single step.

4. Maintain a strong, clear portfolio showing the type of work you want to do.

When I'm reviewing an application, the first thing I do is look at the artist's portfolio. I want to get a sense of the artist from their art before I spend valuable time reading the details of their resume or application. Disney/Pixar's John Lasseter has often said, "Quality is the best business plan, period." So true.

5. Establish a continuing education plan for what you want to master.

Sketch, learn, read, practice, and be disciplined. Volunteer to teach a short workshop at a local elementary school, or at church (when you teach others, you always learn more yourself). Keep growing as an artist.

6. Hustle, promote, and network

You need to market yourself. Go to events, and network with other artists. There is no substitute for face time and building relationships. Where relationships are formed, opportunities are made.

This can be hard for many creatives because we tend to be introverts (to one degree or another). Embrace it and face it. You'll be glad you were stretched and it gets easier over time as you gain experience.

Be sure to leverage high profile projects and build on successes. One success leads to another. Set up twitter and linked in accounts. Join local and national industry groups in your creative area.

7. Persevere and enjoy the journey!

Freelancing is hard work. But it's worth the effort. Take the long view and don't let the end game be your only focus. Living a full life includes enjoying the journey as you pursue your goals. Honestly, I'm writing this to myself right now. Creatives need constant reminders that the goal isn't the real purpose, the journey itself is!

Here are 2 Tips for How To Have A Constant Flow of Freelance Work

It's an ongoing process. There are always peaks and valleys. Serving 3-4 clients well and trying to build lasting relationships is key.

As I mentioned previously, a freelancer is their own company. Every company has a specific bandwidth based on number of employees and how many production hours each employee has to give. As a freelancer, you have to figure out your bandwidth, and budget your time accordingly. Even with best laid plans though, it's still messy. You'll have a quiet week waiting on clients to approve something, then you'll have all of them approve the next step at the same time. There will be 3 hour days and there will be 13 hour days. You try to manage it, but sometimes it's inevitable.

A constant flow of work comes with serving clients well over time. For a freelancer (or small business for that matter) it takes time to build up enough clients to have a constant flow of work. There are no short cuts because trust is built one project at a time and most clients don't have work to send you every week. There are 2 key factors in generating workflow consistency. They are:

1. Marketing

The creative landscape is a crowded space. There are thousands of artists to choose from and it's your job to get on the radar of enough clients to sustain your career. The good news is, once you find a niche market or two and determine to stake a claim there, you can begin to market to those clients with laser focus.

Here's more good news. Most marketing is free. Marketing simply means promotion. Any way you can find to promote you and your services is marketing. You can start a linked in page, online portfolio, YouTube of Vimeo channel, Facebook fan page, or any other form of social media you choose. Those are great, but the real marketing comes when you target a market and start researching who the players are. Then you focus on trying to connect with potential clients thru social media, industry events, and the like.

2. Customer Service

It's one thing to land a client. It's another thing to keep them. It's your job to build trust with clients as you serve them well. You want to make sure they are pleased with the process and the product. If the experience of working with you is unprofessional, discourteous, or communication challenged, chances are you just secured a one-off project. It takes way more work to initially connect with a client than it does to keep them, so treat them well and your chances of them returning the next time they need your creative services increases exponentially.

Tips on How To Handle Taxes as a Freelancer

As an independent contractor, you are responsible to estimate and pay your own taxes (usually 4 times per year unless you are just starting out). If you work for a company, they take taxes out for you, but as a freelancer (or small business owner) you have to do this yourself. Don't worry, this sounds scarier than it really is. One disclaimer here: I'm an artist and an entrepreneur, not a tax specialist or a CPA so please contact one before you implement any of this advice.

I highly recommend finding a good CPA (Certified Public Accountant) to help you with this. They can give you guidance on how to track your expenses, estimate quarterly taxes for federal and state payments, and help keep you on track with all things tax related. It's really not that difficult, especially when you have a CPA. This also gives you an added level of professionalism and protection.

If you are just starting out, ask around to see what CPA's your friends or family use. You can also check your local Better Business Bureau or Chamber of Commerce to see what CPA's are listed in your area. Meet with a recommended CPA (or 2 or 3) in person to ask questions and see if you feel like they are a good fit to help you.

You should expect to pay a few hundred dollars per year for CPA tax planning as a freelancer. It's money well spent to keep you on track and to allow you to spend your time generating income.

There are 2 basic things you need to track as a freelancer: income, and expenses.

We use Quickbooks for my company. It's pretty easy to set up a company with it and begin tracking income and expenses. There are other software packages to use or you can even track income and expenses in a spreadsheet to give to your CPA. I prefer Quickbooks because you can send estimates and invoices to clients with it and you can generate several different types of reports to give to your CPA and for your own planning purposes.

The purpose is to track income and expenses so you can deduct expenses from the income to determine a final income amount you need to pay taxes on. For a freelancer, this is tied to your personal taxes so there are many factors which vary from person to person because of factors like tax bracket, marital status, dependents, and geographical location.

As a general rule, when I'm budgeting projects I assume 25-30% will ultimately go to taxes. Ouch. Yes. That hurts. Embrace it. Again, your CPA will help you with quarterly tax planning (which means once every three months you pay a chunk of taxes to federal and state), but it's good practice to set aside 25-30% of every payment you receive to have for taxes. The last thing you want to do is get to the end of the year and find out you owe more than you have set aside. Been there. Done that. Not fun.

CHAPTER 17

Indie Life

Creativity takes courage.

Henri Matisse

Some artists and freelancers thrive on service work. They enjoy just working on creative projects in their field, hitting deadlines like a Ninja, and getting paid for what they do.

Other artists want to be more creatively independent, working solely on their own ideas and making a living by selling art.

For many, it's a combination.

You have to pay the bills while working on the dream.

A few years ago, we went to the KidScreen Summit in New York City to meet with people from several kids networks. The week before we went, I saw a blog post by brand and marketing guru Seth Godin about Tim Burton's many "failed" attempts before AND in between his green lit projects.

While in Manhattan, we stayed 1 block away from MoMA (the Museum of Modern Art) where it just so happened that a temporary Tim Burton Exhibit was on display featuring art from his high-school days thru the present. It was amazing to see how many different mediums

Tim Burton worked in. There were illustrations, mobiles, sculptures, live action films, animated films, experimental art, and more.

One notable part of the exhibit (that reminded me of the Seth Godin post) was a huge wall that had all of Tim Burton's movie concepts listed. Next to each was it's year of release OR a phrase like "Never Produced", and other similar phrases. MOST of his projects had that term next to them. "Never Produced."

We should not feel like we have failed when we have that stamp on one of our projects or ideas (unless it was never produced because we never tried to ship it). "Never Produced" used to have a negative connotation, but now means to me "Never Giving Up" and "Learning and Preparing for the Next Step."

As I mentioned in an earlier chapter, I could point to many "failures" at Timbuktoons that prepared us for something bigger. Our goal should be "to attempt great things", not to, "to try something only if you have a 100% chance of success". Where's the passion and adventure in that proposition? A real adventure is not complete with out some scratches and bruises along the way. No story is compelling without the scene where hope is almost lost. Never give up, even if you "fail often!"

Practical Tips for Creative Independence

The four main ingredients for creative independence are:

1. A marketable service, and

2. Margin for your own creative ideas (even if you don't sell them)

3. Persistence

4. Passion

You need a marketable service to make a living wage and reach your financial goals. You need to make it a priority to work on your own creative ideas, even if it's just for your own creative health. There will be some "not so creative or fun" projects you work on because people are paying you. Make sure you maintain some level of creative independence to work on art that comes from your soul.

There are some great ways for even struggling artists to work on their own projects. There are websites like Patreon.com where you can solicit patrons (people supporting specific artists) to support you as an artist (as opposed to sites like KickStarter.com that support a project). Of course there's good old fashioned elbow grease where you carve out time to work on your projects.

I have worked on this book on and off for 8 months. I use Evernote (evernote.com) so I can access a file no matter where I am. I've written chapters of this book on my iPhone, computer, and iPad, in doctor's offices (I have 3 kids so that's more common than you might think), at soccer fields during my kid's practices, at night if I happen to wake up with an idea, and in the bathroom (don't judge me).

The point is, you have to be passionate, persistent, and disciplined to work on your own creative projects. Goal setting is key (more on that in a later chapter).

Now that I've flooded your brain with (hopefully) a bunch of inspiration, ideas, and potential for creative plans, let's get specific. Let's determine where you currently are and where you want to go.

CHAPTER 18

You Are Here.

---

*If people knew how hard I worked to get my mastery,
it wouldn't seem so wonderful at all.*

Michelangelo

Think of your career map as one of those large backlit directories just inside the entrance of your local mall. There is usually a red dot that reads "You Are Here."

Take a minute to write down a sentence describing (to the best of your ability) where you currently are in your creative development and career. Use the formula below.

You Are Here.

I am *(level of certainty)* that I want to be a(n) *(list position or career goal)* in the short term, and a(n) *(list position or career goal)* in the long term. I have *(number)* year(s) *of (type of training)*, and *(number)* year(s) of work experience as a *(current position)* toward this goal.

For example: I am **80% certain** that I want to be a **background designer** in the short term, and a **production designer** in the long term. I have **two** years of **college level art** training, and **one** year of work experience as a **jr. layout artist** toward this goal.

Notice that there is a logical connection between the training, experience, and positions stated. This will help you see if your training and work experience need to be adjusted to reach your long term goal.

Also, notice that I didn't attach years to either goal. I want you to think more broadly and generally right now. We're trying to get to the core of your calling and creative passions so we can then set some specific goals.

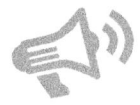

DOING THE WORK

I saw the angel in the marble and carved until I set him free.

Michelangelo

I boxed for a few years during high school and early in college. I noticed how some boxers just took fights to get a pay check but had no real long range plan.

I remember watching an interview of one particular boxer talking about how he planned his fight strategy for each fight, how he trained for each fight, and how he planned his career as a whole including who to fight and in what order.

He had a goal (to become the undisputed champion) and planned his career based on that goal. He had a simple motto (which I'm sure wasn't originally from him) which I've found both simple and profound. "Plan your work. Work Your Plan". Simple words with a ton of hard work behind them. In order to work your plan, you're going to need some really S.M.A.R.T. goals!

CHAPTER 19

S.M.A.R.T. Creative Career Goals

You'll fail at 100% of the goals you don't set.

Mark Victor Hansen

Once you are clear on your calling, you set goals, plan your work, then work your plan. In order to plan, you have to set S.M.A.R.T. goals. I was introduced to this goal setting system last December when I went through Michael Hyatt's five-day goal setting course. Prior to that my goals were usually missing one of these 5 very important components, but I didn't even realize it. This simple system took my goal setting to an entirely new level.

S.M.A.R.T. goals are:

1. **Specific:** Your goals must be clear and detailed, not broad, general or vague.

2. **Measurable:** You must be able to measure progress toward your goals.

3. **Achievable:** Your goals must be realistic and attainable.

4. **Relevant:** Your goals must matter. They must line up with your overall plans and strategy.

5. **Time-bound:** Your goals must have a time frame and a target date or deadline.

I honestly didn't know how powerful each of these components was until I implemented them into my goals this year. I have been setting goals for years, however I have found this method to be revolutionary. I wish I would have learned it years ago. It's amazing what one small pivot can accomplish in a short time.

What I've found is that even some great goal setters and achievers, are missing one of these components. Leaving one component out won't kill your goal setting but it weakens it's effectiveness. This method just flat out works.

Here are examples of 3 of my goals for 2014. Two are professional goals and one is a personal goal. Notice the specificity of each and see if you can confirm that each of the 5 S.M.A.R.T. components are present.

Identify my thought-leadership niche and start a blog by January 31, 2014

(I launched my first post on January, 15th 2014 and the blog has already gone through two major alterations.)

Write and release a thought leadership e-book by September 30th, 2014.

(At the writing of this chapter it looks like I'll launch the e-book before in August of 2014.)

Plan and go on an adventure that helps others and is physically demanding by July 31st, 2014.

(I went on a mission trip to the Dominican Republic with my oldest son in June, 2014.)

For the sake of transparency, I have also missed a goal. I had planned to write and illustrate a children's book this year as well. The skill of goal setting is a process of learning how to make sure your goals are **Realistic**. That goal by it's self is realistic, but I discovered that all four goals together in the same year (along with client work, being a soccer dad and running a company) were not. Realistic goal setting helps temper ambitions so that we don't take on too much at once. This skill, like any other, is honed and refined as you use it.

What I have learned is that it is better to have one to three goals that you can complete with a level of excellence, than it is to have too many goals that risk being half-baked or completely unobtainable. I also learned the importance of prioritizing goals so that the goals with the most important impact, or that are most strategic, are completed first. Pushing less strategic goals off until next year is not the end of the world.

If you have been taking notes in a journal, this would be a great time to get it out and turn to a new page for a goal setting exercise.

Again, think of this book as a funnel. Look thru all of your previous notes about your personality type, core values, identity, calling, creative flavor, "You Are Here" statement, then brainstorm some potential goals. If you are a person of faith, I recommend praying through and praying for your potential goals.

Goal Setting Exercise

1. Take some time to list five to seven goals (in all areas of your life, not just professional) that you would like to accomplish in the next year. Spend time rewriting them with more specificity until all five S.M.A.R.T. goal components are present.

2. Once you have a draft of your five to seven goals, share them with someone you trust and get some feedback.

3. Refine and finalize your goals.

4. Put them somewhere you will see them every day.

5. List the next single step toward each goal and put a due date next to it.

6. As you complete an action step, write the next single step along with a due date. Rinse and repeat.

Remember that the only way to move a mountain is one shovel full at a time, and the only way to eat an elephant is one bite at a time. Start digging and start chewing and before long you'll see yourself moving closer and closer to your creative career goals.

CHAPTER 20

Master Your Craft

---

*A winner is someone who recognizes his God-given talents,
works his tail off to develop them into skills, and uses these skills
to accomplish his goals.*

Larry Bird

At this point you've done the tough soul-searching work of figuring out your identity and calling (or at least you've read about it this far which says a lot). You've written your "You Are Here" statement so hopefully at this point you clearly see the gap between where you are and where you want to be. You have established your S.M.A.R.T. goals and identified your immediate action steps.

I like to make things as practical as possible so I have another exercise I would like for you to do. First, get the spiral notebook or sketchbook that you've been journaling in and on a new sheet of paper write down 10 things you need to work on (in terms of marketable skills) to help you get from where you are to where you want to be. What additional skills are needed for that future position you desire?

Stories put skin on principles, so I'll share another quick personal story to help illustrate what I mean here. If you'll recall my career transition story earlier in the book, there was a point where I knew that

I had officially fallen in love with visual development and all things animation.

I had the confidence I could do it, but I didn't have the portfolio to show it (sometimes entrepreneurs believe they can do things they have never done before. Even Steve Jobs famously had a "reality distortion field"). So, I set out to develop a portfolio that showed I could be a visual development artist. I used every spare moment to develop concepts around characters and worlds. Then I used as many different mediums as possible to create different types of art depicting these characters and worlds. I acted as if I were really developing them for a feature film.

If you don't have an opportunity make one. If you don't have the level of skill needed, work on it. It takes discipline, work ethic, boldness, and a small bit of insanity (just enough to make you attempt great things.)

Years later, I'm still working in visual development and producing animation. The hard work and persistence pays off. I'm still not the artist I want to be but I still draw regularly and I'm still growing as an artist.

Once you pick a direction, put the work in. Make it a daily discipline. In the book Outliers, author Malcolm Gladwell shows it takes 10,000 hours to master any craft. Start logging hours.

CONCLUSION

Never give in. Never give in. Never, never, never, never — in nothing, great or small, large or petty — never give in, except to convictions of honor and good sense.

Winston Churchill,
Entire 1941 Harrow School speech

The game has its ups and downs, but you can never lose focus of your individual goals and you can't let yourself be beat because of lack of effort.

Michael Jordan

You are here for a purpose. You were born an artist for a reason. It's your job use what you've been given to make the world a better place. This is the best time ever to be an artist and there are more opportunities than ever for the one who is willing to work hard, be disciplined, bold, and courageous.

It's time to take the next step in your creative journey as you further discover your artistic voice, and live out your identity and calling. The best part is when you do this you will thrive. That doesn't mean it's an easy road or that opportunities will fall into your lap. It does mean if you follow your calling you will be in the zone like never before.

A good friend of mine pointed out that we are human beings, not human doings. Never forget that you have a calling because of who you are, not what you do. Roles, seasons, and assignments will change, but pursue your creative calling in every role you find yourself in and watch the journey unfold one step at a time.

Remember that the creative life is 1% inspiration and 99% perspiration. Never doubt the initial spark of inspiration as you push thru the hard work that's necessary to make good on your creative goals.

Your long-range goals may shift as opportunities arise and unexpected detours occur, but be sure to use your identity, calling, and core values as guides for your decisions.

You are called as an artist. Your skills are needed at this time in history. Your leadership and courage are paramount. When you are able, be sure to help those coming behind you by freely sharing information and knowledge from your experience. You'll be glad you did. Please join me in this worthy task of Calling All Artists!

ACKNOWLEDGEMENTS

If you love life, don't waste time,
for time is what life is made up of.

Bruce Lee

First and foremost, I want to thank my Lord, who pursued me when I was far from him and transformed my life to one of purpose.

I want to thank my wife Tracey, who has listened to me babble on about this book, and who has wrangled the kids and put up with my late night writing so that I could finish the book this summer. Thank you for believing in me always, and for using your skills and training as a language arts teacher to proof read this manuscript (and your skills as a wife to know when I need encouragement).

I want to thank my children Daniel, Natalie, and Luke, who give me inspiration and a sense of purpose and adventure every day.

I want to thank my Dad and Step-mom for encouraging me and for supporting my artistic and entrepreneurial pursuits. Dad, I have learned, and still learn, so much from you.

I want to thank my Mom, who was always so proud of every little accomplishment and who unexpectedly went to be with the Lord in January. I miss you.

I want to thank my sister Corinne, and step-brothers Barry and Andy, for the fun times growing up, for our adult friendships, and for encouraging me as an artist.

I want to thank my friend Charlie Bancroft for helping me nail down my calling, as well as Sean Copley and Nate Pope, my "Inkling" brothers, for their encouragement and wisdom over the past year, and Brett Laxton, my long distance creative comrade.

I want to especially thank each of my friends in this book, who contributed their time and passion for art and mentoring others, by allowing me to interview them and put a slice of their life in these pages.

I want to thank Phil Vischer, who gave my fledgling studio a shot when he started the "What's In the Bible?" series, and for a timely pep talk when I had to lay some close friends off last year. You were right. The passion and creativity came back.

Last but not least, I'd like to thank Pastor Bobby, Steve, Ben, Jennifer, Justin, Bryon, Nathan, and the rest of the staff and friends at Journey Community Church for fostering an environment of creativity and service to others, and for creating "The Perfect Church for Imperfect People" where my family has thrived like never before.

S. D. G.

RESOURCES

Below is a list of books (by category) that I have personally read, benefited from, and recommended to friends. Some are old. Some are recent. All are relevant and will impact you on your journey. These are all books that have personally impacted me in a profound way. Most of which, I've read more than once. I highly recommend each one.

Creativity/Art Direction/Visual Development

Creativity Inc., by Ed Catmull

The Pixar Touch, by David A. Price

The Visual Story, by Bruce Block

Framed Ink, by Marcos Mateu-Mestre

The Art of Rise of the Guardians, by Ramin Zahed

Animation/Comics/Cartooning/ Character Design

The Animator's Survival Kit, by Richard Williams

Action Cartooning, by Ben Caldwell

The Art of Silver, by Stephen Silver

Creating Characters With Personality, by Tom Bancroft

Pose Drawing Spark Book, by Cedric Hohnstadt

Business and Leadership

Creativity Inc., by Ed Catmull

Good to Great, by Jim Collins

The 21 Irrefutable Laws of Leadership, by John Maxwell

Start With Why, by Simon Senek

The Animation Business Handbook, by Karen Raugust

Necessary Endings, by Henry Cloud

StandOut, By Marcus Buckingham

Purpose/Identity/Calling

The Purpose Driven Life, by Rick Warren

Experiencing God, by Henry Blackaby

One Big Thing, by Phil Cooke

Wild at Heart, by John Eldredge

Growth

The Circle Maker, by Mark Batterson

All In, by Mark Batterson

In a Pit With A Lion On A Snowy Day, by Mark Batterson

Church Strategy and Branding

Deep and Wide, by Andy Stanley

Biographical/Autobiographical

Me, Myself, and Bob, by Phil Vischer

www.ingramcontent.com/pod-product-compliance
Lightning Source LLC
Chambersburg PA
CBHW051806170526
45167CB00005B/1895